AIR CAMPAIGN

THE HUMP 1942–45
America's first massive military airlift

MARK LARDAS | ILLUSTRATED BY GRAHAM TURNER

OSPREY PUBLISHING
Bloomsbury Publishing Plc
Kemp House, Chawley Park, Cumnor Hill, Oxford OX2 9PH, UK
Bloomsbury Publishing Ireland Limited,
29 Earlsfort Terrace, Dublin 2, D02 AY28, Ireland
1385 Broadway, 5th Floor, New York, NY 10018, USA
E-mail: info@ospreypublishing.com
www.ospreypublishing.com

OSPREY is a trademark of Osprey Publishing Ltd

First published in Great Britain in 2025

© Osprey Publishing Ltd, 2025

All rights reserved. No part of this publication may be: i) reproduced or transmitted in any form, electronic or mechanical, including photocopying, recording or by means of any information storage or retrieval system without prior permission in writing from the publishers; or ii) used or reproduced in any way for the training, development or operation of artificial intelligence (AI) technologies, including generative AI technologies. The rights holders expressly reserve this publication from the text and data mining exception as per Article 4(3) of the Digital Single Market Directive (EU) 2019/790.

A catalog record for this book is available from the British Library.

ISBN: PB 9781472865946; eBook 9781472865953; ePDF 9781472865922; XML 9781472865939

25 26 27 28 29   10 9 8 7 6 5 4 3 2 1

Maps by www.bounford.com
Diagrams by Adam Tooby
3D BEVs by Paul Kime
Index by Fionbar Lyons
Typeset by Lumina Datamatics Ltd
Printed by Repro India Ltd.

Title page: see caption on p. 24.

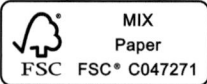

Osprey Publishing supports the Woodland Trust, the UK's leading woodland conservation charity.

To find out more about our authors and books, visit www.ospreypublishing.com. Here you will find extracts, author interviews, details of forthcoming events and the option to sign up for our newsletter.

For product safety-related questions, contact productsafety@bloomsbury.com

Author's note:
This book describes events that occurred in the middle of the 20th century, from the early 1930s to the mid-1940s. The world was a different place then, with different attitudes, different boundaries (political and cultural) and very often, different names.
I have used the period names in this book along with the political divisions of that era. Chungking and Canton for Chongqing and Guangzhou; India for what is now India and Bangladesh; and Burma for Myanmar. Similarly I report period attitudes as they existed, not as we wish they would be.

The following abbreviations indicate the sources of the illustrations used in this volume:
AC – Author's Collection
LOC – Library of Congress, Washington, D.C.
NARA – National Archives
NMUSAF – National Museum of the United States Air Force
USNHHC – United States Navy Heritage and History Command

AIR CAMPAIGN

CONTENTS

INTRODUCTION	4
CHRONOLOGY	9
ATTACKER'S CAPABILITIES	12
DEFENDER'S CAPABILITIES	24
CAMPAIGN OBJECTIVES	33
THE CAMPAIGN	42
AFTERMATH AND ANALYSIS	88
FURTHER READING	93
INDEX	95

INTRODUCTION

Japan invaded Burma to cut the Burma Road by taking Rangoon and Mandalay. Yet once the Japanese learned the British were building an airfield in Myitkyina, the Imperial Army moved into Upper Burma, taking the airfields at both Myitkyina and Lashio, pushing the airlift route north to the Himalaya foothills. (AC)

In 1937 Japan and China went to war with each other for the third time in under 50 years. The First Sino–Japanese War of 1894–95 established Japan as a regional power; potentially as an emerging great power. It cost China Taiwan, the Penghu Islands, and the Senkaku Islands, ceded to or seized by Japan. It led to Korea's independence from China and China's eclipse as a regional power.

Japan sealed its great power status in the Russo–Japanese War of 1904–05, defeating Russia, annexing Korea, and expanding its Chinese influence. In September 1931 Japan used the Mukden Incident, self-inflicted damage to the Japanese-controlled South Manchuria Railway, as a pretext to declare war on China. In a five-month war, it wrested control of Manchuria from China.

Initially established as the "independent" State of Manchuria in 1932, Manchuria became a monarchy in 1934. In reality, Manchukuo (as Japan called it) was a Japanese puppet state, run by Japan for Japan. It provided Japan with a frontier for exploitation and expansion. Previous wars of aggression having served so well, Japan decided to start one more.

In 1937 they again declared war on China. The pretext was the Marco Polo Bridge Incident on July 7. The Japanese used a shooting incident and an AWOL Japanese soldier as an excuse to invade (the private returned before battle started). Japan expected to carve off another piece of China with another short, victorious war.

Initially things went well. Japan captured Shanghai in September and China's capital, Nanking, in December. Having scooped up Northern China, the Japanese waited for China's Kuomintang government to surrender, ending the war. Instead, China's government, led by Chiang Kai-Shek, relocated to Wuhan, and continued fighting. After the Japanese took Wuhan in 1938, Chiang relocated the government to remote Chungking in Western China.

The Japanese moved into territory controlled by Mao Tse-Tung's Communist insurgency. One reason for Chinese weakness in the 1930s was civil war between the Kuomintang Nationalist government and the Communists. The Nationalists gained the upper hand

Japanese tanks roll through the streets of Shanghai in September 1937, at the beginning of the Second Sino–Japanese War. Japan expected the war to end quickly, before the end of 1937. Instead, they found themselves trapped in a quagmire which they could not win and could not end. (USNHHC)

and forced the Communists into Northern China, territories now held by Japan. While the Communists continued warring with the Nationalists, they fought the Japanese, too.

Japan was in a war it could not win and could not end unless they could force China's surrender. The Kuomintang government, aware it was too weak to expel the Japanese, but also aware China was too big for Japan to occupy, continued fighting. It hoped to exhaust Japan before they, themselves, became exhausted. Meanwhile Kuomintang and Communist forces continued fighting each other and the Japanese.

China needed weapons to fight. Japan occupied most of China's industrial areas by 1938. China still produced small arms and ammunition, but depended on foreign imports for artillery, armor, and especially aircraft. In 1937 and 1938 China used aircraft donated by the Soviet Union. By 1939, especially after the 1939 Molotov–Ribbentrop Pact between the Soviet Union and Nazi Germany, Moscow lost interest in China. To lead China away from the Soviets, military aid from the West was forthcoming, especially from the US. It supplied aircraft, and by 1941 permitted organization of the American Volunteer Group.

Turning a blind eye to its own neutrality laws, the US allowed China to recruit volunteer pilots from the US air forces, Army, Navy, and Marines. Volunteers were allowed to resign from the US Armed Forces to serve as Chinese mercenaries. They were provided aircraft and allowed to secretly train at an airfield near Lashio, a town in British-held Burma.

Japan began a campaign cutting China off from the outside world, stopping the weapons flow. Between May 1938 and June 1940 it captured all important ports held by Free China and closed all but one route through neutral territory: the Burma Road.

INTRODUCTION

OPPOSITE STRATEGIC OVERVIEW

By the summer of 1941 the Burma Road was China's last remaining logistical connection to the outside world. It was narrow and rough. As shown here, trucks could barely negotiate its one lane. Regardless, Japan wanted to shut it down, for morale purposes as much as strategic intent. (LOC)

This was a railroad–road connection running from Burma to Kunming, capital of China's Southwestern Yunnan province. Chiang negotiated an agreement with Britain to build a road connecting Kunming with Lashio, a town in Burma's Northeastern Shan State. Britain believed an overland route to China would benefit Burma's economy. Lashio connected by rail to Rangoon, Burma's principal port. From Lashio, cargoes could be trucked to Kunming on a single-lane graveled road built between 1937 and 1938.

Although the straight-line distance from Lashio to Kunming was 348 miles, the Burma Road ran 717 miles. It cut through rugged mountain terrain creating a winding path with multiple switchbacks. Traffic traveled one-way with the direction alternating depending on the week. A one-way trip took ten to 14 days to complete – if there were no bridge washouts or rockfalls to be cleared.

Even the Burma Road closed in July 1940. Germany invaded and conquered France in June 1940. Britain, facing Germany and Italy alone, shut down the Burma Road in July 1940 due to Japanese demands. Only a few commercial flights by China's national airline, China National Aviation Corporation (CNAC), connected China to the world. Formed in 1930, and by 1933 40% owned by the US Pan American Airways, it was still making flights to Hong Kong.

Japan's aggressions in China annoyed the US. The US press was sympathetic to China due to the efforts of US Christian missionaries in China and Henry Luce. Luce owned *Time* magazine, a major US news weekly. Born in China to US missionaries, Luce led the pro-Kuomintang China Lobby. Additionally, Franklin Roosevelt, then President of the US, was favorably inclined towards China. His maternal grandfather, Warren Delano, made his fortune in China trading tea and opium. Grandson Franklin held a romanticized view of China's potential. Japan's aggression outside China created the real alarm, though.

In September, Japan signed the Tripartite Pact with Germany and Italy, entering a formal military alliance. France, under the Vichy government, was a junior partner. It was forced to permit Japanese occupation of Tonkin, Indochina's northernmost province.

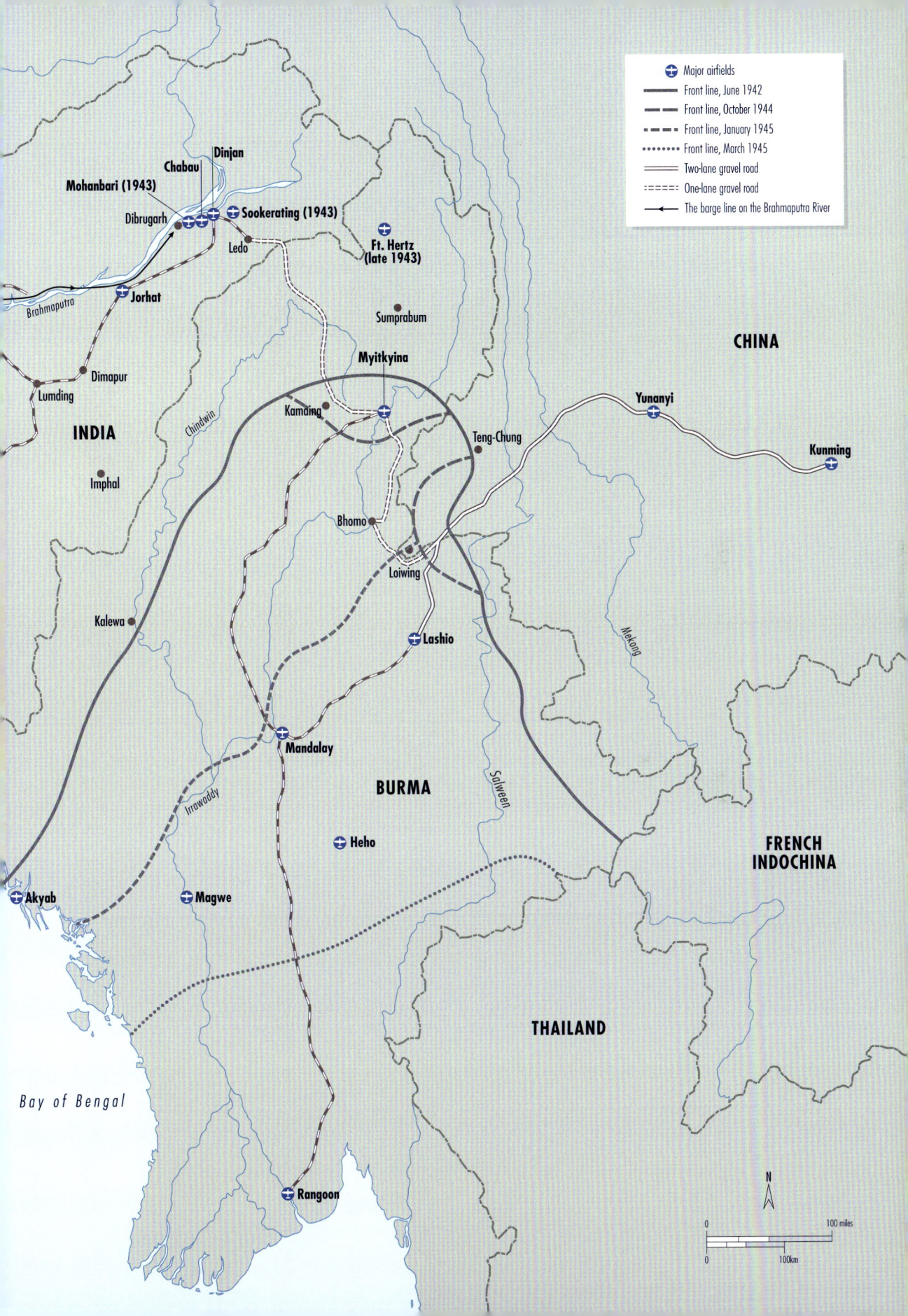

Moving into a European colony by occupying Northern Tonkin raised the stakes. Britain and the Netherlands had colonies in the region. Their concern was Japan would not limit itself to Axis colonies, but would seize those of other European powers. The US controlled the Philippines, just across the South China Sea from French Indochina. The US planned to grant the Philippines independence in 1946, but did not wish a former colony to be occupied by Japan. Following the US lead, Britain and the Netherlands sought to reign in Japanese aggression. The US responded by embargoing scrap iron sales to Japan. Britain reopened the Burma Road.

This failed to deter Japan. It occupied all French Indochina in June 1941. Matters quickly slid to war. The US froze Japanese assets in the US, demanding Japan evacuate Indochina. When Japan refused, the US embargoed petroleum sales in July 1941. Britain and the Netherlands quickly joined the embargo.

This gave Japan's economy and military nine months before both ran through oil reserves and ground to a halt. Japan decided to go to war and take needed resources by force. On December 8 Japanese time (December 7 east of the International Date Line, including the Continental US and Hawaii), Japan launched a surprise, multi-pronged attack against US, British, and Dutch interests throughout Asia and the Pacific, igniting the Pacific War. This included an attack at Pearl Harbor, which crippled the US Pacific Fleet.

Over the next month Japan invaded the Philippines, the Dutch East Indies, British holdings in the Malay Peninsula, and numerous US and British possessions in the Central Pacific. They seemed unstoppable. Now keeping China in the war was more important than ever. One million Japanese soldiers were tied down in China. If China made a separate peace, these troops would be freed to be used against the US and Great Britain.

The only remaining supply line was the Burma Road. It was quickly being shut. Japan invaded Burma on January 1, 1942. By March, Japan occupied Rangoon, cutting the Burma Road. By June, Japanese invaders held Lashio. China was cut off.

Yet a new supply line was already under development. The same day Japan invaded Burma, T. V. Soong, Kuomintang's finance minister (and Chiang Kai-Shek's brother-in-law), wrote proposing a new supply line. This one would be aerial. Airfields in Assam were only 550 miles from Kunming. Could not, Soong asked, they be used to fly supplies to China? Soong further wrote that CNAC had already surveyed a route, stopping at Myitkyina, Burma en route to Kunming.

Roosevelt approved the concept. Within a month wheels were already turning to turn Soong's request into a reality. In April 1942 the first flights from Assam to Yunnan began. It followed a different route, further north than the one Soong originally proposed. Myitkyina had fallen to Japan. The new route flew over the Himalaya foothills, towering mountains, or alternately over the still unoccupied jungles of Upper Burma. Because of the height and ruggedness of the terrain, the passage soon acquired a name, "The Hump."

It took time to fix the problems and turn the effort into an effective and efficient airlift. Yet over the next 44 months, the US Army Air Force would accomplish something no other national air force managed up to that time: a successful, long-term resupply of an isolated army by air. This is how it was done.

CHRONOLOGY

1930
July Chinese National Aviation Corporation (CNAC) formed.

1933
Pan American Airlines purchases 45% of CNAC.

1937
July 7 Second Sino–Japanese War begins.

1940
September 22–26 Japan occupies Tonkin and Northern French Indochina.

September 27 Japan signs the Tripartite Pact with Germany and Italy.

October 16 US President Franklin Roosevelt imposes an embargo of scrap iron and steel exports to Japan in retaliation for Japan's occupation of Tonkin.

November CNAC's manager conducts survey flights from China to Burma and Assam, India.

1941
July 26 Roosevelt embargos petroleum sales to Japan and freezes Japanese assets in the United States in retaliation for the announced movements of Japanese troops into all of French Indochina.

July 28 Japan sends 140,000 troops to French Indochina in preparation for invading the Dutch East Indies.

December 7 Japan attacks the US Pacific Fleet in Pearl Harbor, and concurrently attacks British, Dutch, and US Far East holdings.

December 21 Thailand signs a treaty of friendship with Japan, effectively declaring war on the Allied powers.

1942
January T. V. Soong requests aerial resupply of China using the Assam to Kunming route. He asks for 12,000 tons of supplies monthly.

January 22 Japanese forces cross the border into Burma from Thailand.

February 12 The Tenth Air Force is activated at Patterson Field, Ohio, and assigned to India, including responsibility for the China airlift.

March RAF engineers begin work expanding Dinjan Airfield in Assam and building an aerodrome in Myitkyina.

March 7 Britain evacuates Rangoon, cutting the Burma Road.

To enhance the chances of survival if downed, all aboard a Hump flight were issued "blood chits," like the one shown here. The chits carried the flag of Nationalist China for recognition and asked for help for and protection of the bearer. Some offered substantial rewards for assistance. (NMAF)

March 20 The Assam-Burma-China Ferry Command is organized as part of Tenth Air Force, and allocated 25 CNAC transports.

April 9 First Hump flight. Three C-47s carry 100-octane aviation fuel to Kunming to refuel Doolittle raiders.

May 8 Japanese occupy Myitkyina.

July 15 Ferry Command becomes the Air Transport Command

September Franklin Roosevelt pledges to send 500 warplanes to China and airlift 5,000 tons of supplies each month.

September 22 First fatality on a Hump flight. A C-53 disappears with all hands 90 minutes after departing Kunming. The plane and crew are never found.

October 25–28 Japanese bombers and fighters attack US airbases at Dinjan, Chabua, Sookerating, and Mohanbari.

December 1 The Tenth Air Force 1st Ferry Group becomes the India-China Wing of the ATC.

1943
January First C-87s arrives in India.

March Fourteenth Air Force activated in China.

May 25 The Trident Conference immediately increases the monthly quota of supplies to be flown into China to 7,000 tons and 10,000 tons by September 1943.

May First C-46s arrives in India.

August 9 Operation *Tsuzigiri* begins, with Japanese fighters hunting Hump transports.

September Colonel Thomas Hardin takes command of airlift operations to China.

October 25 Search and Rescue Squadron formed at Chubau to find downed aircraft and rescue crews.

October 27 Operation *Tsuzigiri* fighters fall into a trap and are ambushed when they mistake B-24s for C-87s.

October 31 Operation *Tsuzigiri* cancelled.

November 18 First bailout from a Hump transport. They return to Allied lines 23 days later.

December 31 Monthly cargo carried exceeds 10,000 tons for the first time.

1944
March 6 Operation *U-Go* begins.

April 2 First B-29 arrives in India.

April 3–16 Battle of Kohima.

April 26 First B-29s arrive in China.

May 17 Allied forces capture Myitkyina airfield, fly in reinforcements.

June 15 B-29s attack Yawata, Japan from bases in China.

June 22 Allies reopen the Kohima–Imphal road, *U-Go* ends.

August 3 Allied forces capture the city of Myitkyina.

September Thomas Hardin departs ICD, replaced by William Tunner.

October ICD adds C-54s to its inventory, and begins using them on the airlift.

October 19 General Albert Wedemeyer replaces Stilwell as US commander of the CBI Theater.

December 4 *Grubworm* airlift operation begins.

1945
January 5 *Grubworm* concludes after moving 44,000 Chinese troops.

January 6–7 Severe storm hits the Hump routes. A minimum of 15 aircraft and 31 lives are lost before flight operations are cancelled until the storm passes.

January 12– Feb 4 First convoy travels Stilwell Road from Ledo, India to Kunming, China.

January 17 Twentieth Air Force launches final raid from Chinese airfields, attacking various targets in Kyushu.

August 6 Japan ceases hostilities.

September 2 Instrument of surrender signed aboard USS *Missouri* in Tokyo harbor.

September 21 C-46 flying to China encounters engine trouble and crashes in Mang Shih, China, the last aircraft lost flying the Hump.

November 15 Hump airlift formally closed.

Until the end of 1943 China lacked earthmoving equipment. Airfields were constructed with manual labor. Conscripted workers broke up the rocks used for the gravel paving of runways with hammers, spread them by the bucketful, and leveled them with hand-pulled rollers. In payment they received a bare minimum of food. (AC)

ATTACKER'S CAPABILITIES
Supporting a nation

Militarized Douglas DC-3s were the backbone of the China airlift in its first two years. Their ceiling was too low to fly over the highest mountains on the route. The USAAF mainly used the C-47 Skytrain or the C-53 Skytrooper. This is a C-47; the C-53 had a smaller cargo door. (AC)

The China airlift was an unprecedented campaign. Never before had one nation attempted to supply an army, much less an entire major allied nation, exclusively by air. It required a lot of resources. Aircraft, of course, but not just transports. Warplanes were also required, to protect the transports and airfields and to reverse the Japanese tide that swept over Burma.

A complex infrastructure was also required in order to build airfields supporting the airlift and to feed the supply lines with cargo to take to China. That infrastructure had to support the armies shielding the airlift. Everything became more challenging due to the terrain and the distance of the theater from the United States, where the logistics chain began.

While the objective of this campaign was moving cargo rather than taking territory, the Allies were the ones on the offensive. They had to fly cargo to China. Japan's role was to stop them. When the airlift started, the Japanese occupied most of Burma. The Allies – US, Great Britain, and China – had the task of recovering enough of Burma to secure the airlift. Additionally, the British and their Commonwealth Allies desired to recover all of Burma from Japanese occupation.

The terrain included high mountains and dense undeveloped jungles, some of the most difficult fought over in World War II. Additionally, it involved coalition warfare, with three allies – the US, China, and the British Commonwealth – with widely divergent strategic goals. Tactics had to be developed to fit the available weapons into the unique conditions of the theater. To understand how and why the Allies accomplished what they did, starts with an understanding of the attacker's capabilities.

Aircraft

Although both warplanes and transports participated in the China airlift, the featured aircraft were the transports. Five types were used: the DC-2/C-32 and C-33, the C-47 and C-53, the C-46, the C-54, and the C-87/C-109. Curtiss manufactured the C-46, Consolidated the C-87 and C-109, and Douglas made the rest.

Douglas DC-2, C-32, and C-33: A low-wing, twin-engine transport originally developed as a 14-passenger civilian airliner in 1934, it had a top speed of 210mph and cruised at 190mph. Its ceiling was 22,500ft, but was designed to operate below 10,000ft. It was unpressurized. Oxygen was required above 12,000ft. It carried two tons of cargo 1,000 miles. CNAC used these extensively before World War II and flew them on Hump routes, including the first survey flight. The US military impressed 24 civilian DC-2 passenger airliners into service as the C-32, and 18 of the cargo version as the C-33. Some of these were used on the Hump.

Douglas C-47 Skytrain and C-53 Skytrooper: The C-47 was a militarized version of the twin-engine, 21-passenger DC-3 airliner. It first flew in 1938. C-47s had a strengthened floor, cargo door, cargo hoist attachment, and a tail cone permitting a glider to be towed. The C-53 was a militarized transport version of the airliner, without the reinforced floor, cargo door, and hoist attachment. It had 28 seats for passengers. Both had two 1,200hp Pratt & Whitney R-1830-90C Twin Wasp 14-cylinder air-cooled radial engines.

Their top speed was 224mph, and the cruising speed 204mph. They carried three to four tons of cargo 1,600 miles. Their ceiling was 26,000ft, but when fully loaded were hard-pressed to reach 20,000ft. As with the DC-2, they were best operating below 10,000ft. Pilots loved it. It was rugged, reliable, and had forgiving flight characteristics. They participated in the China airlift from the beginning, including the first cargo flights from Chabua to Kunming.

"Cumulogranite"

The deadly combination of mountains and bad weather was a greater threat to the survival of aircrew flying the Hump than the Japanese. The further north you flew, the higher the mountains grew and the wilder the weather became.

One thing feared by Hump pilots was running into a mountain. Pilots called it "cumulogranite", rock mountains hidden behind clouds. Running into a mountain at aircraft cruising speed would stop your clock – and everything else in your airplane. Death was inevitable and instantaneous.

Sometimes miracles happened. One such occasion occurred in April 1943, when a CNAC C-47 flown by C. J. Rosbert and "Ridge" Hammell ran into bad weather while flying home to Kunming from Assam. It was a first trip across the Hump for Hammell. Rosbert was a seasoned veteran of the trip. Their aircraft ran into heavy rain shortly after takeoff. As the airplane climbed, they met fog and snow. At 12,000ft their aircraft iced up. The windshield soon accumulated a six-inch layer of ice, through which pilot Rosbert could see only a hand-sized gap. The ice began dragging them down.

Flying blind, almost literally, they would have been safe had they been flying their intended course. Unknown to them, crosswinds had blown them far north of their intended flight path, into the towering Mishmi Hills. These loomed up higher than the heavily ice-laden C-47 could fly. Suddenly, at the last minute, Rosbert spied an oncoming cliff, dead ahead and close by.

Desperate to avoid the mountain, Rosbert yanked the controls into a steep bank but was too close to avoid hitting the mountainside. His desperate bank put the wings parallel to oncoming rocks; however, instead of smashing into the mountain nose first, the aircraft skimmed along the treetops, effectively making a forced landing at 180mph on a runway banked 45 degrees. This illustration shows their predicament just before they dropped down onto the mountain.

Rosbert and Hammell survived the unconventional landing. The radio operator was killed, thrown from his seat and breaking his neck. They were 16,000ft high, lost in the Himalayas. Both survivors were injured, Hammell with a twisted ankle, Rosbert with a broken leg. They spent three days recovering in the airplane. The next day they started climbing down the mountain.

It took them two weeks to find help in a small village of Stone Age Mishmi tribesmen. They proved friendly, taking the pair to a larger village better able to take care of them. After two weeks there, a runner was sent to a British scouting column nearby. After another 13 days, the pilots were recovered by the British. It took another 16 days to hike from the village to British lines. Seven weeks after they ran into the mountain, they were back in Assam. During that time they had traveled 270 miles to return home. The flying time from their Assam starting point to the crash site was 90 mins.

16 ATTACKER'S CAPABILITIES

Despite a high ceiling and generous cargo capacity, the C-87 Express was unloved by most fliers. In his memoirs Ernest Gann stated, "It was said the assembly of parts known collectively as a 'C-87' would never replace the airplane." Its most dismaying characteristic was inability to fly if experiencing icing. (LOC)

Consolidated C-87 Express and C-109 Liberator: The Express was a transport version of the B-24 Liberator bomber. The turrets and bomb bay were faired over, and a solid nose with a cargo hatch attached. The cargo floor was strengthened, and ran through most of the aircraft. The C-109 was a tanker conversion of existing B-24 heavy bombers. The armor and armament were removed and eight fuel tanks installed in the body.

Both had a top speed of 300mph and a cruise speed of 215mph. The service ceiling was 28,000ft and flew easily at 20,000ft, even fully loaded. It could fly 1,400mi fully loaded. The C-87 carried up to nine tons of cargo on Hump flights, while the C-109 carried 2,900gal of fuel as cargo. (Both aircraft also carried 2,900gal in wing tanks.)

Neither was popular with flight crews. It had difficulty taking off fully loaded from runways 6,000ft above sea level, had wretched climb characteristics, and lost lift when experiencing icing. Author and pilot Ernest Gann, who flew the aircraft, stated they "could not carry enough ice to chill a highball." The C-109's fuselage tanks often leaked, leading to gas vapor explosions. Gann claimed pilots called it the "C-one-oh-boom." The aircraft's main virtue was availability. The first C-87 arrived in January 1943.

Curtiss C-46 Commando: This was a twin-engine transport originally developed as a high-altitude pressurized civilian airliner. It used a deep fuselage with a figure-eight cross section, a floor at the intersection of the two arcs, and the wing spar directly under the floor. It was intended to carry 34 passengers in the upper half with the bottom half used for cargo. Curtiss failed to interest airlines in the aircraft, and failed to develop a pressurization system before it entered production. In 1940, the Army Air Force saw its potential as a military transport, placing an initial order in September 1940.

The Commando was powered by two 2,000hp Pratt & Whitney R-2800-51 Double Wasp 18-cylinder radial engines. It had a top speed of 270mph, a cruising speed of 173mph, and a 3,150mi range at cruising speed. It carried six to seven tons of cargo, twice that of the C-47. It had a service ceiling of 24,000ft and could fly comfortably at altitudes above the Lower Himalayas of the northern Hump routes, despite lacking a pressurization system.

Despite its advantages, pilots generally disliked it. Pressed into service before resolving development problems, it was hard to fly, mechanically unreliable, and required massive maintenance to keep flying. It also tended to explode midair. Pilots were afraid to turn on

The Curtiss C-46 Commando could fly higher and faster than the C-47 with a larger payload using the same crew. Untested when it first appeared on the airlift in March 1943, it possessed significant flaws. These caused frequent crashes until corrected. It took a year for the Commando to become reliable. (NMAF)

the heaters lest they spark an explosion. The cause was only discovered postwar: the wing was unvented and fuel leaking from the wing tank pooled in the wing root and vaporized. Thirty-one C-46s exploded flying the Hump. C-46s first appeared at the Hump in May 1943.

Douglas C-54 Skymaster: Developed from another Douglas passenger liner, the four-engine DC-4, this was the US's best transport during World War II. Under development prior to US entry into the war, the prototype first flew on February 14, 1942. The military took over all orders from civilian airliners, and had Douglas produce it as a military transport. The version most commonly used for the China airlift was the C-54D, introduced in August 1944.

This version used four 1,100hp Pratt & Whitney R-2000-9 Twin Wasp 14-cylinder radial engines. It had a top speed of 275mph and a cruising speed of 190mph. At cruise speed it could carry ten tons of cargo 4,000mi at 20,000ft on four engines.

Pilots loved it. Gann called it "a wonderful machine," one that "could carry a great deal of cargo *and* ice." Its weakness was its three-engine performance, which limited its altitude to 15,000ft, lower than the peaks of the Lower Himalayas. It was not used on the Hump routes until autumn 1944, after the Japanese were cleared out of Northern Burma, and the lower, southern routes were safe to fly without fear of Japanese interception.

The warplanes used by the Allies to support the China airlift were largely US-made. China got all its aircraft from the US, and Britain and its Commonwealth associates used US aircraft in this theater. Later Britain relied extensively on the US Army Air Force in theater.

Fighter aircraft present included the Curtiss P-40 Warhawk (including various export versions), the Republic P-43 Lancer, the Vultee P-66 Vanguard, and the North American P-51 Mustang. All four were single-engine, low-wing, all-metal monoplanes with retractable landing gear. The first three were developed in the late 1930s; they represented the first generation of the all-metal monoplane.

The P-40 was the standard US Army fighter when the US entered the war, and had been widely exported before then, including to China and Britain. The famous "Flying Tigers" flew P-40s. The P-43 and P-66 were built for export and sent to China because they were available, and were wanted by no one else. All three could hold their own against Japanese aircraft, if just barely. The P-51 was the best US fighter of the war. It arrived in theater in late 1944 and dominated the air.

Three bombers were widely used: the twin-engine North American B-25 Mitchell, the four-engine Consolidated B-24 Liberator, and the Boeing B-29 Superfortress. The Mitchell was one of two standard US medium bombers in World War II, while the B-24 was the more advanced of two standard US heavy bombers. The B-25s provided much of the tactical air support for Allied forces, while the B-24 was used against strategic targets. Late in the war, as Japanese targets grew scarce, both ferried fuel and supplies to China.

The Superfortress was a super-heavy strategic bomber. The USAAF intended to base it in China to attack targets in Japan. It played a part in the China airlift during 1944 as its bases were the destination for fuel and supplies carried to China. The bombers were stationed in India, and staged to China to attack Japan.

A final category of warplane playing a role in the airlift was liaison aircraft. High-wing, light aircraft capable of landing on short, unimproved runways, these were used to recover downed aircrew.

Facilities and infrastructure

The China airlift illustrated the adage that amateurs talk tactics while professionals talk logistics. Not only was the airlift a logistics effort, but logistics and available infrastructure dominated the ability for the airlift to bring supplies to China. Everything from the airfields used to the spare parts used to maintain the aircraft had to be built on the spot or brought from the United States over a 15,000mi supply route. It was a logistician's and engineer's campaign.

The transport airfields used were improvised at the beginning of the airlift and constantly improved throughout the campaign. Transport aircraft, even those as basic as the C-47, could not operate long on unimproved grass runways. Paved surfaces were required, at minimum, macadamized gravel with or without cement binders. These were lacking when the airlift started.

Kunming, capital of Yunnan Province, had a prewar airfield capable of handling multi-engine transports. There were 23 other airfields in Yunnan, including one at Yunnanyi that was expanded during the airlift. The British had one airfield in Assam Province when Japan attacked in 1941, at Chabua, built in 1939.

The British hastily carved a second at Dinjan, initially responding to Japan's invasion of Burma. Completed in March 1942, the USAAF used it as the western terminus of the airlift. Dinjan was quickly followed by two more: Mohanbari and Sookerating. Sookerating, initially built in 1942 to base fighters, was expanded to house C-46s in early 1943.

During the early years of the airlift, all Hump airfields were primitive. Initially only runways were paved; generally only parts. The remaining runways and taxiways and stands

In China, massive stone rollers, like this one on display at the National Museum of the Air Force, leveled gravel runways at airfields capable of taking heavy bombers or transports. They were pulled by workers. A worker who slipped and fell while pulling was often crushed by the roller. (William Lardas)

were rammed earth or gravel. Living quarters and operational buildings were based on local Assam huts called *bashas*. Sometimes personnel were housed in tents. Barracks had beaten dirt floors and were often miles from the airfield. There was no running water. It had to be pumped into storage tanks serving the latrines and showers. Food was bad. Conditions improved, but not until mid-1944.

One of the Allies' great strengths was their engineering capabilities. Massive numbers of construction and combat engineers were sent to the CBI between 1942 and 1944. These men were used to improve infrastructure. They built airfields. By the time of the spring 1944 Japanese and summer 1944 Allied offensives, Allied combat engineers could drop into a bridgehead held by airborne forces or infiltration forces (such as the Chindits or Marauders), carve out a crude airfield overnight, and quickly improve it to take C-47 and C-46 transports. Transports then flew in construction equipment (to improve the airfield) and heavy weapons (including artillery) to secure the bridgehead from counterattack. Aerial resupply of isolated Allied forces became routine.

Engineers also built roads and pipelines, improved facilities (especially those involved in logistics) and improved housing. By 1943, aviation fuel reached the Assam airfields by pipeline from Calcutta, eliminating the need to use barges or rail to ship it. By January 1945 the pipeline system reached Kunming.

That pipeline followed the Ledo Road to the Burma Road and from there to Kunming. The Ledo Road was another massive engineering project. It started at Ledo, India, the terminus of the Indian railroad system. It cut through Burmese jungles until it reached Loiwing on the Burmese-Chinese border. There it merged with the old Burma Road, cut in spring 1942.

Infrastructure projects in India and Burma used mechanization. In China runways and roads in were largely constructed by conscripted Chinese peasants. They broke rocks by hand, filled runways with them, by wheelbarrow, and used massive hand-drawn stone rollers to compact the surface. Conscripts were poorly housed, poorly fed, and rarely paid. Even the massive B-29 fields constructed in 1944 used virtually no mechanized tools.

The terrain between Assam and China over which the aircraft flew formed part of the infrastructure. There were several routes to reach Kunming from Assam. The northern route took aircraft over the Himalaya foothills. These ranged in height from 8,500 to 16,000ft. Despite rumors (and the fears of the pilots) no peak reached 20,000ft over the northern Hump route. Yet even a 16,000ft mountain made this route problematic for the Douglas transports. Safety dictated an altitude at least 2,000ft higher than the highest peak expected.

The weather over this route was some of the world's worst. Warm, moist monsoon air from India collided with dry, frigid air from the Himalayas and Tibetan Plain. The result was monstrous thunderstorms, severe icing conditions, and powerful wind shears. Icing was exacerbated because aircraft departing the Assam airfields in the Brahmaputra basin were leaving a hot, humid environment.

The southern route, which flew just north of Fort Hertz, was lower, but altitudes of 8,000ft were common.

The airlift required massive engineering effort to build the airfields supporting the airlift. The CBI Theater also involved major engineering projects to build the Ledo Road and gasoline pipeline alongside it. The equipment used was eclectic, ranging from modern bulldozers to the region's traditional earthmover: elephants. (AC)

Supplies traveled by rail to reach the airlift airfields. Originally, goods traveled across India from Karachi and later from Calcutta. Regardless, the last leg of the journey was a narrow-gauge railroad in Northern Assam, complete with the need to use a railroad ferry to cross the Brahmaputra River. (AC)

Kunming, the Chinese terminus of the airlift, was 6,900ft above sea level. This route was easily within the 10,000ft altitude at which the Douglas transports were happiest. Yet pilots were reluctant to use the southern route, especially in 1942 and 1943 due to fear of meeting Japanese fighters. Additionally it required flying over seemingly impenetrable jungle. Pilots feared this more than the mountains. They believed if they hit a mountain they would die quickly. If they bailed out over the jungle, they would slowly starve to death or be killed by local wildlife.

In reality, the jungle's indigenous peoples were generally friendly to the Allies. They would rescue downed Hump fliers, and hold them until they could be recovered and returned to their bases. The US eventually developed a sophisticated recovery service, using light aircraft to fly downed pilots out of jungle villages.

To reach China, supplies first had to reach Assam. That involved a supply line that ran at least 11,000 miles by sea and railroad and up to 15,000 miles from the US East Coast to the Assam airfields. In 1942 and 1943, before it was safe to send cargo ships through the Mediterranean, ships carrying cargoes for China departed ports from Southeast Atlantic ports, typically Norfolk, Charleston, or Savannah. From there they sailed around the Cape of Good Hope to Karachi (now part of Pakistan, but then part of India). Starting in early 1944 they could knock 4,000 miles off the sea leg by going through the Mediterranean and traversing the Suez Canal to reach Karachi.

Cargoes were offloaded and loaded onto railcars. From there they traveled by rail 1,550 miles to Assam, where they were unloaded at the four airlift airfields. Alternatively, they were taken by rail to Calcutta, loaded onto barges, and carried by barge up the Brahmaputra River to Dibrugarh. From there cargoes could be trucked to Mohanbari (next to Dibrugarh) or taken by rail to Chubau, Dinjan, or Sookerating. Only then could they be loaded onto transports and flown 500 miles to Kunming.

Rail traffic was complicated because different Indian provinces and princely states used different railway gauges. Whenever the width of the track changed, cargoes had to be unloaded from one set of boxcars and loaded on a new one, a process that often took days. An item could take up to 48 days to travel by sea from America, spend an additional week being unloaded from ship at Karachi, and then another two to three weeks wending across India on boxcars or barges before reaching Assam. The flight was the fastest and shortest leg of the trip.

Light, high-priority cargoes or aircraft capable of long-range flight being ferried to the CBI could fly from the US to Assam or on to China. The USAAF established a regular service to move spare aircraft parts to Assam to keep the transports flying. The route was over 12,000 miles and took a week to ten days, depending on the time spent on the ground. Of that, 60 to 72 hours were spent in the air.

Weapons, electronics, and tactics

USAAF transports were unarmed. They carried no weapons because transports were generally not supposed to fly into hostile territory. When they did, they depended on either stealth or armed warplanes for protection.

The warplanes were armed with a variety of weapons, including .303, .30cal, and .50cal machine guns, 20mm autocannon, and bombs of different types. Most relevant was the

.50cal machine gun, carried by both USAAF bombers and fighters. It was the weapon used most frequently for air-to-air combat. It, along with 250, 500, and (occasionally) 1,000lb bombs, were also used for ground support.

The USAAF used the Browning M2 .50, a highly reliable, air-cooled machine gun. Aircraft used a dedicated aircraft version, the AN/M2. The M2 had a muzzle velocity of 2,910fps. It could fire 750 to 850 rounds per minute. The gun fired a 52-gram bullet, capable of penetrating one inch of armor and was capable of penetrating structural steel of unarmored ships. It was potent against ships, ground vehicles, buildings, and other aircraft. Japanese aircraft used in this campaign, poorly armored and frequently lacking in self-sealing fuel tanks, were vulnerable to this weapon.

More relevant to the airlift than the weapons which transports did not mount was the navigation and communications aboard the transports, and the electronic navigation and early warning systems used at airfields and ground bases in the theater.

The electronics aboard the transport aircraft were primitive. Most had just a magnetic compass, a gyrocompass, and a radio. Some, most notably the C-109, were equipped with radio direction-finding (RFD) antennae, which provided the direction of the broadcasting station.

The only radio navigation aid available to aircraft without RFD systems was Low Frequency/Medium Frequency Radio Range navigation. This used ground stations. They broadcast a repeating 30-second signal between 200 and 410kHz, below that of commercial AM radio. It opened with a six-second Morse code identifier for the station followed by a continuously repeated Morse "A" (dit-dah) or "N" (dah-dit), depending on the quadrant.

On two opposite quadrants, it broadcast "A," with the "N" signal broadcast on the adjacent quadrants. In a three-degree-wide cone at the quadrant intersections, the "A" and "N" overlapped. This was called "the beam." Instead of a dit-dah or dah-dit, the pilot heard a solid tone. If the beacon was at the destination airfield, a pilot could "follow the beam" until the airfield came into sight.

A pilot could also use the signal as a navigation point. Since the location of the broadcast station was known and the angle of the beams known, it gave the pilot a bearing to the station. Used with other navigation information (time, compass heading, airspeed, and estimated winds aloft), it could fix the airplane's position. RFD provided similar bearing information and could be used in a similar manner. Neither LF/MF nor RFD provided range information, however.

When the airlift started, only Chabua had an LF/MF station. This allowed Assam-bound aircraft to quickly find a landing field, even if lost. This was important, because returning aircraft had limited fuel. Kunming gained a beacon next, by 1943. Eventually Fort Hertz had one. Through much of 1943 this was the sole navigation waypoint on the Hump route, allowing transports an opportunity to fix their position midway in their flight. From mid-1944 on, especially after the Allies gained air superiority, stations were added to Burmese airfields like Myitkyina.

The transports, especially those available in 1942, lacked sophisticated navigation equipment. Although the C-47 was considered advanced by 1930s–40s aviation standards; yet its cockpit navigation aids consisted of a magnetic compass, a gyrocompass, a clock, and a radio. In 1942 many C-47s lacked a direction-finding antenna. (NMAF)

OPPOSITE FLYING THE BEAM

The only radio navigation available in World War II was known as Low-Frequency Radio Range Navigation. Stations broadcast a directional signal 190 to 535kHz starting with a Morse code station identifier every 30 seconds. This was followed by repeated Morse "A" (dot-dash) in two opposite quadrants and "N" (dash-dot) in two other quadrants. At the intersection of the quadrants, the "A" and "N" merged into a continuous tone (the beam). Pilots could navigate by locating and flying the beam.

LF/MF stations averaged a maximum range of 100 miles, although this varied due to weather conditions, time of day, and atmospheric conditions. In bad weather (when most needed) it was frequently less. Sometimes it had a much longer range, which might fool a crew flying too far north into believing they were over lower mountains because they could hear a station. Since the route from Assam to China was over 500 miles, continuous LF/MF radio navigation was impossible until autumn 1944 when stations were added to Burmese airfields and the southern flight route predominated.

Radar gave the airfields a defensive advantage that grew as the war progressed. Initially air defense in India depended on ground observers, who reported enemy aircraft and their direction to a central station for processing. This gave a five-minute warning to the Indian airfields. As radar was installed at the different airfields, that warning period expanded to 30 minutes, long enough to prepare an appropriate reception. By the start of 1944 radar was standard at the Indian airfields. By the time the Allied counteroffensive began that summer, portable radar sets were available. They were installed at the advance Burmese airfields.

Methods of flying the Hump and logistical approaches fell into the category of tactics for campaign purposes. One of the earliest examples of airlift tactics was the policy of having transports fly to China fully fueled and loaded, but only giving returning aircraft enough fuel to reach Assam with a slight reserve for contingencies. Extra fuel in the aircraft after arrival in China was drained down to the reserve. This allowed more fuel, always critically short in China, to remain in China. It was unpopular with the crews because unexpected headwinds could leave an aircraft short of fuel approaching Assam – to the point where reaching a runway was impossible. Only after a fuel pipeline reached Kunming in 1945 was this relaxed.

Until the formation of the Air Transport Command in December 1942, airlift traffic was ad hoc, an adjunct to Tenth Air Force operations. Its commander occasionally commandeered China-bound cargoes and airlift aircraft for his own needs in India and Burma. This stopped after the ATC took charge. It ran the operation as a pilot-run airline, with pilots flying when they chose and along their choice of routes.

This changed in October 1943, when Thomas Hardin took command. He centralized operations. After that, only headquarters could close the route due to weather or enemy activity. Thereafter pilots flew as ordered or risked disciplinary action. As the war progressed, airlift operations continued to grow more structured and more professional.

Ground stations like this one were run by the Army Airways Communications System. They were used to communicate with flight crews, especially during takeoff and landing. In early 1943, there were only nine stations located across the entire CBI. By May 1944, there were more than a hundred stations like this one. (NMAF)

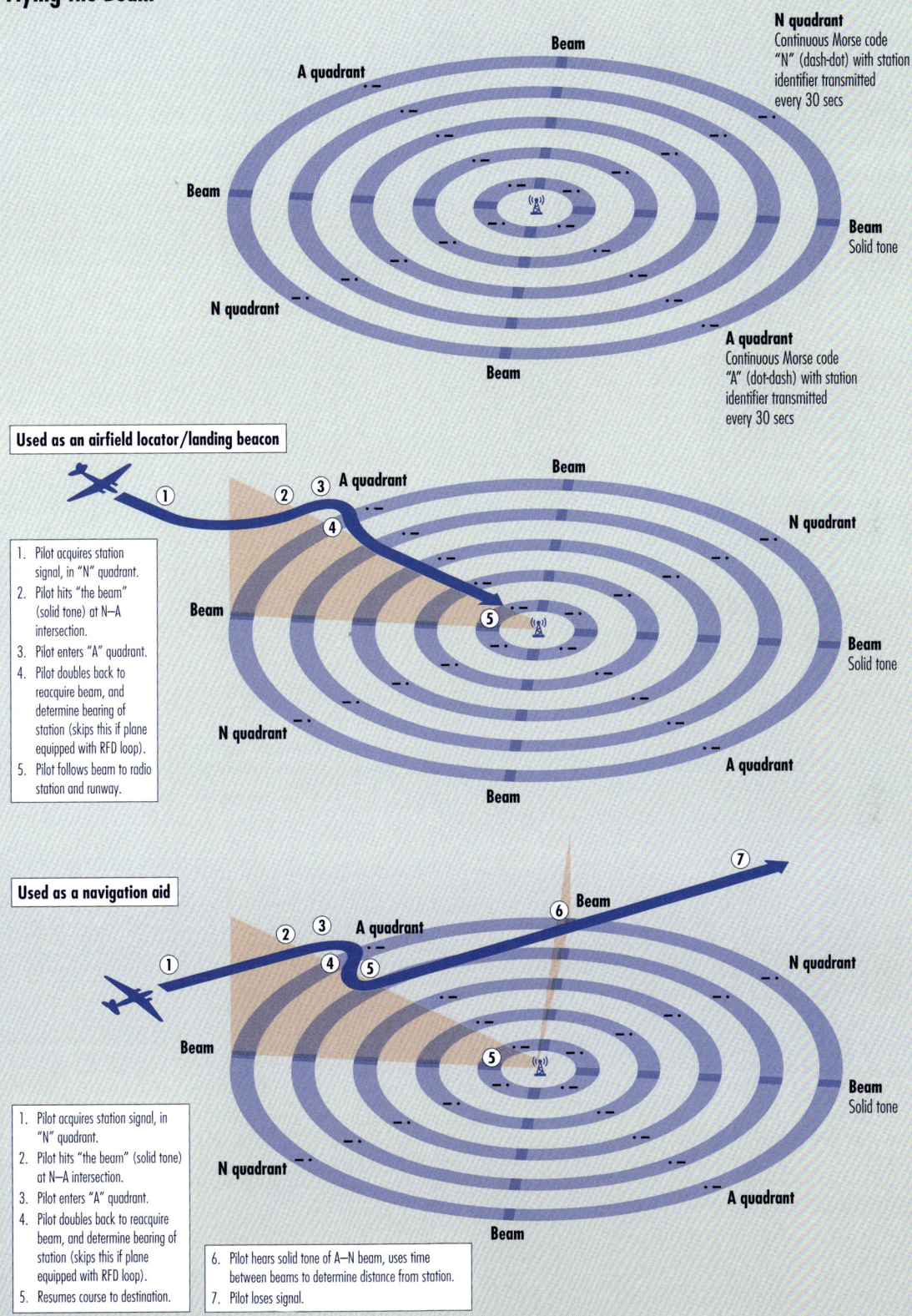

DEFENDER'S CAPABILITIES
Destroying the supply lines

The Mitsubishi Ki-21 was the IJA Air Force's main heavy bomber when the Pacific War started. First operational in 1938, it was elderly by aircraft standards in 1941–42. It remained a frontline aircraft until 1945. It did good service in Burma in 1942 and 1943, including bombing the Assam airlift airfields. (Wikipedia)

For the Japanese, Burma and the surrounding territories in India and China were an all-Imperial Japanese Army show. The Imperial Japanese Navy provided sealift at the beginning of the invasion of Burma, but the action related to the Chinese resupply took place well inland, in Burma's Shan State and Kachin Province. The adjacent Assam Province in India and China's Yunnan Province were equally landlocked. There was plenty of scope for the Imperial Army, but little for the Imperial Navy.

Japan invaded Burma to sever the final supply line running from the outside world to China – the Burma Road. Since this was an overland route, the Japanese assumed that ground forces were sufficient to isolate China. The Imperial Army Air Force units sent to Burma were those intended to support a ground army. Their mission was to seize local air superiority and provide air support to ground forces. This was a well-worn path for the Imperial Japanese Army, one well-practiced in China.

When the US replaced the Burma Road with an airlift, the mission of the Imperial Army and Imperial Army Air Force shifted to interdicting this new supply line. It did not change resources available. No new aircraft and few new ground troops were sent to Burma. The Imperial Army was tasked with stopping a strategic airlift with a tactical air force made up of tactical bombers and relatively short-range fighters. It was ill-matched for the task.

They had significant land forces in theater. To an extent, they attempted to cut off the airlift using ground forces. They invaded deeper into Burma than initially intended, and then attempted to cut off the Assam airfields by taking Southern Assam. This task was constrained by the available aircraft, the facilities and infrastructure in theater, and the weapons and tactics at hand. The Japanese forces in Burma were at the very end of a very long supply line.

This was especially true in the regions most critical to cutting off the airlift, Northern Burma and inland Assam. The primitive road and rail system made supply of Japanese air and land forces there difficult. While the Allies supplied troops by air, Japan lacked the aircraft necessary to do so. Japan's resources were far more constrained than that of the Allies (especially the United States). They were fighting a battle for which they were unprepared.

Aircraft

At the outset of the Pacific War, Japan assigned one air division, the 3rd Hikoshidan, to support the Imperial Japanese Army in Malaya and Burma. When the war began, it consisted of some 360 aircraft of all types. This included types being phased out: the Nakajima Ki-27 fighter (Allied code-name Nate or Abdul) and the Mitsubishi Ki-15 (Babs) attack bomber/reconnaissance aircraft. Most of it consisted of more modern aircraft, the Ki-43 Hayabusa fighter (Oscar), the Mitsubishi Ki-21 heavy bomber (Sally and Gwen), and the Kawasaki Ki-48 (Lily) and Mitsubishi Ki-46 (Dinah) reconnaissance aircraft.

Over the next two years, despite increasing Allied air power, the 3rd Hikoshidan was not reinforced. Replacement aircraft fell behind attrition rates. By January 1944, the 3rd Hikoshidan was down to 277 aircraft: 124 fighters and 153 bombers. These were mainly the newer types present in 1942, mainly the Ki-43, Ki-21, and Ki-48. The obsolescent types were either withdrawn or shot down. A few newer aircraft types were present, notably the Kawasaki Ki-45 twin-engine heavy fighter. Yet it was still largely dependent on the generation of aircraft in production when the war began. Due to Burma's relatively low priority, later war aircraft, such as the Ki-61 Hien and Ki-84 Hayate fighter or Ki-67 Hiryu bomber were never assigned to Burma.

Fighting late-war Allied aircraft with early war Japanese aircraft left the IJA on the wrong end of the air superiority balance. By July 1944 Allied aircraft owned the skies over Northern Burma and by January 1945 Japanese air forces had been evicted from Burma. Thereafter it played no role in stopping the airlift. While it was active, the burden of stopping the airlift fell on three aircraft types: the Ki-43 fighter and Ki-21 and Ki-48 bombers.

Nakajima Ki-43 Hayabusa (Peregrine Falcon – Allied code name Oscar): This was the IJA Air Force's standard fighter aircraft at the start of the Pacific War. The Royal Thai Air Force, allied with Japan in this campaign, also used Ki-43s. First flown in 1939, it was the IJA's first all-metal, enclosed-cockpit fighter with retractable landing gear, replacing the fixed-gear Ki-27. It entered production in April 1941.

It was a single-engine monoplane, powered by an air-cooled radial engine. Early-war versions had a 14-cylinder 1,150hp Nakajima Ha-114 engine; late-war aircraft carried a 1,250hp Mitsubishi Ha-33 engine. The early war aircraft (the type predominantly used in Burma) had a top speed of 495km/hr (308mph) at 4000m (13,125ft). It had a ceiling of 11,750m (38,500ft) and a maximum range of 1,200km (745mi).

It was a relatively short-legged aircraft. To intercept transports flying the airlift or attack the Assam airfields, they had to either operate from airfields in Burma's Northern Kachin state or accept extremely short times over target. It did have two under-wing attachment points and could carry two 200l (44gal) drop fuel tanks, which extended the range up to 72 percent. It lacked armor or self-sealing fuel tanks.

It was indifferently armed. The aircraft operating out of Burma generally carried either two 7.7mm Type 89 machine guns, or one 7.7mm and one 12.7mm Ho-103 machine gun, or two 12.7mm Ho-103 machine guns. This made shooting down even an unarmed transport a challenge. The Hayabusa had superior flying characteristics compared to Allied aircraft present in Burma when the war began, but was inferior to later generation Allied aircraft such as the P-51 or P-47. Even earlier in the war, their indifferent armament allowed aircraft like the P-40 to fight at relatively even odds.

Mitsubishi Ki-21 (Allied code-names Sally and Gwen): This was the IJA's standard heavy bomber at the start of the Pacific War. The Allies would have classified it as a medium bomber. It had only two engines and a maximum bombload of 1,000kg (2,250lbs), but it was the heaviest bomber in the IJA inventory in 1941. As with the Ki-43, it belonged to the first generation of all-metal, retractable-landing gear Japanese warplanes.

It was recognizable due to a long dorsal greenhouse, housing a hand-held machine gun over and behind the wing. When this was replaced with a power turret, the Allies initially

The Kawasaki Ki-48 (Allied code name Lily) was the IJA light bomber when war with the US and Great Britain started. Newer than the Ki-21 and faster, it was too slow to avoid fighter interception and too weakly armed to drive them off. It was effective only when there was no aerial opposition. (Wikipedia)

assumed this a new design, hence two code names: Sally (greenhouse version) and Gwen (dorsal turret version).

It entered production in 1938, remaining the Army's first-line bomber throughout the war. It had a maximum speed of 432km/h (268mph) at 4,000m (13,125ft), a service ceiling of 8,600m (28,215ft), and a standard combat range carrying a 750kg bombload of 1,500km (932mi).

The Ki-21 Mk I, of which 424 were built between March 1938 and November 1940, were powered by two 850hp 14-cylinder air-cooled Nakajima Ha-5 KAI radial engines. The Ki-21 Mk II (1,280 built between December 1941 and September 1944) carried two 1,450hp Mitsubishi Ha-101 14-cylinder air-cooled engines. The Mk II had a top speed of 486km/hr (302mph) and a 10,000m (32,810ft) ceiling.

The Ki-21 had a single 7.7mm Type 89 machine gun in flexible hand-held mounts in the nose, dorsal, and ventral positions and one on either beam, aft of the wing. The dorsal mount was later replaced with a powered-turret-mounted 12.7mm Ho-103 machine gun. It had a crew of five: pilot, co-pilot, navigator/bombardier, radio operator/gunner, and gunner. It was extensively used in Burma. In 1942 and 1943 it was used to attack the Assam airlift airfields.

Kawasaki Ki-48 (Allied code-name Lily): This was the IJA's standard light bomber in 1941–42. Development started in 1938 and it entered production in July 1940, with 557 being built between July 1940 and July 1942. An improved version, the Ki-48-II, went into production in April 1942. Before production ceased in October 1944, 1,408 were built. Most of those in Burma were probably the Ki-48-I.

It served a role analogous to that the Douglas A-20 filled for the USAAF, a light attack bomber. The Ki-48-I had a normal bombload of 300kg (661lbs), a maximum speed of 480km/hr (298mph), a service ceiling of 9,500m (31,170ft), and a range of 1,980km (1,230mi). The Ki-48-II carried 400kg of bombs (882lbs), had a maximum speed of 505km/hr (314mph), a service ceiling of 10,100m (33,135ft), and a range of 2,050km (1,274mi). The Ki-48 was another all-metal monoplane with retractable landing gear and an enclosed cockpit. It replaced the Ki-2, an aircraft that entered service in 1933 and was obsolescent by 1940.

The Ki-48-I had two 14-cylinder 950hp Nakajima Ha-25 engines; the Ki-48-II was powered by two 14-cylinder 1,150hp Nakajima Ha-115 engines. Both were radial, air-cooled

The Nakajima Ki-43 Hayabusa (Peregrine Falcon), Allied code name Oscar, was the Imperial Japanese Army's first fighter with retractable landing gear. An all-metal monoplane, it was fast and agile for an early-war fighter. It was also too lightly armed and too lightly protected to be a truly effective fighter. (Wikipedia)

engines. Both versions had a crew of four: pilot, navigator/bombardier, radio operator/gunner, and gunner. It was armed with three machine guns: single hand-held, flexible 7.7mm Type 89 machine guns mounted nose, ventral, and dorsal positions. The final production version of the Ki-48-II replaced the dorsal 7.7mm gun with a single 12.7mm Ho-103 machine gun.

The Ki-48 had no protection for the crew or fuel tanks, depending on speed and maneuverability for safety. It was highly maneuverable; a pilot could loop it. While one of the fastest bombers when it first appeared, fighters reached its speed by 1941, and well exceeded its top speed by 1943. At that point it was approaching obsolescence. The 3rd Hikoshidan started the Burma campaign with two Ki-48 *sentai* (groups), and they remained active in Burma and India until Japan's air forces were chased out in 1944.

Facilities and infrastructure

Japan's effort to stop the aerial resupply of China was constrained by the available facilities and infrastructure. It was complicated because it had to conduct the campaign from Burma, which it invaded in January 1942. By July Japan and its Thai ally occupied most of Burma. Only a strip of the Northern Kachin State was still occupied by the Allies. Japan controlled all prewar airfields, railroads, and ports (including river ports) in Burma. It also controlled most of the existing roads; its conquest followed the roads and navigable rivers.

Under British administration Burma was largely undeveloped. Most of it was either dense jungle or mountainous terrain difficult to cross, except on roadways. The territory was subject to deluging rains during monsoon season. There were few roads in Burma; they were narrow and unpaved, graveled at best. Burma had one railroad in the area, running from Rangoon on the coast to inland Mandalay. From there it had two branches, one running to Lashio near the Chinese border, and the second reaching north to Myitkyina, capital of the Kachin State.

There were few existing airfields, especially in the Northern Kachin and Shan States. Those that existed had few maintenance facilities. Fuel storage and shade-tree mechanics typified the handful of prewar Northern Burmese airfields. Lashio, where the Flying Tigers were training prewar, had facilities to assemble crated P-40s, but that was as advanced as it got.

That meant the first task faced by the occupying Japanese was to build the infrastructure they were going to use. They improved the existing airfields in Upper Burma, especially the airfields at Lashio and Myitkyina. Myitkyina was especially important because it was best placed to interdict the airlift transports and to stage raids on the Assam airfields. It was also a railroad terminus, allowing easy access to move in fuel and munitions.

At the same time, it was close enough to Allied airfields to be easily attacked. The Japanese lacked sufficient air defense resources to adequately protect it. Instead of stationing aircraft at Myitkyina, the IJA Air Force stationed its aircraft in Lower Burma, where they were maintained and serviced. Only rudimentary maintenance and resupply services were available at Myitkyina – fuel, machine gun ammunition, and the ability to patch up damaged aircraft so they could return to Lower Burma.

Aircraft would stage to Myitkyina, refueling there to conduct operations. This could be bombing the Assam airfields or hunting transports flying between India and China or ground support of IJA ground troops. Once operations concluded, they returned to airfields around Rangoon and Moulmein, which were safe from Allied attacks through 1943.

Nor were Myitkyina and Lashio the only airfields in Upper Burma. It was easy to pick a location with access to local transportation, clear a runway, erect huts to fuel and service aircraft, and operate from there. IJA aircraft could operate from grass runways. Allied intelligence estimated that the Japanese built 20 to 40 of these forward airfields.

Theater infrastructure was just one problem faced by Japan. Logistics was another. Just as Assam and China were at the very end of a US supply line, Burma was at the very end of a Japanese supply line. The sea route from Japan to Rangoon, then Burma's main port, was 4,500nm – a three-week voyage by cargo ship. However, except for a period in early 1942, sea travel to Rangoon was hazardous.

The long voyage along the Andaman Sea to Rangoon gave Allied submarines numerous opportunities to attack ships steaming to and from Rangoon. Most were British or Dutch submarines. During 1942 and 1943 their torpedoes, unlike those of the US through

Burma was at the end of a very long supply line for the Japanese. Initially, all supplies, including aviation fuel, had to come through Rangoon, Burma's principal port. Supply ships had to run a gauntlet of Allied submarines to reach Rangoon, leaving Japanese forces perpetually short of supplies. (NARA)

October 1943, worked. By 1943 Japan was losing a significant portion of the cargoes headed to Burma.

To thwart this, in June 1942 the Japanese began construction of a railroad to connect Bangkok, Thailand to Rangoon. The Thai terminus was Ban Pong, where an existing railroad connected with Bangkok. The Burma terminus was Thanbyuzayat, where a spur of the existing Burma Railroad that ran from Rangoon down the Burmese panhandle along the Andaman Sea coast passed. Roughly 268 miles of mountainous, river-divided jungle separated these points. It was some of the world's most rugged and least-developed terrain.

Work started on September 16, 1942. Using forced labor, including Burmese and Thai civilians and Allied POWs, Japan completed the railroad in just 13 months. The two ends connected on October 17, 1943. The railroad was declared open on October 25. The human toll was horrendous. Over 180,000 workers were employed in its construction. Of these over 100,000 died; an estimated 90,000 civilians and 12,000 Allied POWs. It was called the Railroad of Death, commemorated in the novel *The Bridge over the River Kwai*.

Even this new line, which shortened the sea route from Japan by 1,500 miles, did not ease supply problems. Over the next 18 months 500,000 tons of supplies traveled over the railroad. It sounds like a lot, but breaks down to an average of 28,000 tons per month. In December 1944, the US *flew* 32,000 tons from Assam to China. By October 1943 the problem was twofold: Japan was running out of supplies to send to Burma and running out of ships in which to ship supplies.

Japan had to support intensive fighting on three different major fronts besides Burma: the Central Pacific, the Southwestern Pacific, and China. Its wartime economy was barely big enough to support its commitments in China. The US drive across the Central Pacific and up the Solomon Island chain overtaxed the Japanese military. That made Burma an afterthought. It received what could be scraped up after higher priority theaters were dealt with. There were shortages of everything, especially petroleum products, including aviation gasoline. And aviation gasoline was the lifeblood of any air campaign or air operation.

There was also a shortage of ships in which to move cargoes. By summer of 1943 the United States Navy solved the issues preventing its torpedoes from exploding when they hit. War construction added several score submarines to its Pacific fleets by then. Armed with effective torpedoes, they waged a devastating war on Japan's shipping.

The danger zone was no longer just the Andaman Sea. There were choke points where US, British, and Dutch submarines clustered all along the route from Japan to Bangkok or

A train travels on the Burma-Thai Railroad in 1945. Built in 1943 and 1944 using slave labor, including Allied POWs, it was known as the Death Railroad. There were high death rates among those conscripted to build it. It eliminated the need to ship supplies by sea to Burma. (AC)

Singapore. The resulting massacre of shipping left Japan unable to supply its armies. Too few freighters and tankers remained by the middle of 1944. By December, Allied advances severed the supply line between Burma and Japan at the South China Sea.

Even when it had adequate supplies, in 1943 and the first quarter of 1944, it had no means of moving those supplies beyond the railheads at Mandalay and Myitkyina. There were no roads capable of supplying armies north and west of the rail line. Any attempt to cut off the Assam airfields by a ground offensive had to rely on infiltration tactics, and forgo heavy weapons. Against an enemy that could be resupplied by air, this was futile.

Ultimately Japan had to rely on its air forces to sever the airlift. It simply lacked the number of aircraft – and the fuel – required to do that.

Weapons and tactics

Although the Japanese used land offensives in an effort to stop the China airlift, these never succeeded. Their main effort was in the air. The Japanese tried interdicting transports flying the Hump, and bombing out the Assam airfields from which supply originated. This involved the use of various machine guns and bombs.

The machine guns carried by Japanese aircraft in Burma were the 7.7mm Type 89 machine gun and the 12.7mm Ho-103 machine gun. Most were the Type 89. Initially both fighters and bombers were exclusively armed with the Type 89. Not until late 1942 did aircraft begin to carry the Ho-103, generally one in the dorsal mount for the bombers and either one or two fixed forward-firing guns in the Hayabusa.

The 7.7mm Type 89 machine gun was rifle-caliber, dating to World War I. The fixed version was a licensed copy of the British Vickers .303 machine guns. They were nose-mounted on Hayabusa, synchronized to fire through the propeller arc. It was belt-fed, with a rate-of-fire between 700 to 900 rounds per minute and a muzzle velocity of 820m/s (2,690ft/s).

The flexible version was based on the IJN Nambu T-11 machine gun, itself a modification of the French Hotchkiss M1909 Benét–Mercié machine gun. It had a higher rate-of-fire, 1,400 rounds per minute, and a slightly lower muzzle velocity: 810m/s (2,650ft/s). It was drum-fed, with a 69-round pan.

Both were gas-fed and air-cooled. Both were chambered to fire a 7.7x58mmSR Type 89 cartridge, a rifle-caliber round. The bullet massed 10–12g (depending on the type of round) with an energy between 3,300–3,500J (2,440–2,590ft-lbf). This was satisfactory in the days of open-cockpit aircraft that had wood framing and canvas covering, but by the 1940s most aircraft were metal-framed and covered. A rifle-caliber round lacked the stopping power to easily bring down most multi-engine aircraft.

The Ho-103 12.7mm (.50cal) machine gun was significantly more effective. It, too, was gas-fed and air-cooled. An unlicensed (and unauthorized) copy of the US Browning M2 .50cal, it was introduced in 1941. Chambered for the 12.7x81mmSR Breda cartridge shorter than the one used on the M2, it potentially had a higher rate of fire, 983 rounds

The Type 89 7.7mm machine gun was the standard weapon used by Japanese aircraft in Burma. It fired a rifle-caliber bullet better suited to the 1920s than the 1940s. This picture illustrates the flexible twin mount used in some bombers. Twin-mount Type 89 machine guns were not used in Burma. (AC)

per minute (versus 750–850rpm on the AN/M2 used on US aircraft). However, when mounted to fire through the propeller arc (as it was when mounted on the Ki-43), its rate-of-fire dropped to 400rpm, negating that advantage.

The projectile massed 45 to 51 grams, depending on the round, and had a muzzle velocity of 780m/s (2,600ft/s). It had four to five times the energy as the 7.7mm round. Both fixed guns and flexible guns mounted on the bombers were belt-fed. It was effective against single-engine aircraft, even with just two guns. It was effective against bombers and large transports when four to eight were mounted (as was the practice for the .50cal in Allied air forces). With only two mounted on the Ki-43, it usually took multiple passes to shoot down even an unarmed transport.

Japanese bombers carried four types of bombs when attacking Assam airfields: the Type 94 50kg, the Type 94 or Type 1 100kg, and the Type 92 250kg and 500kg high-explosive bombs. All four had a cast-steel nosepiece connected to a tubular steel body, and a conical steel nosepiece to which four sheet steel fins were welded. All were filled with picric acid explosive, loaded in preformed paraffin-wrap blocks. The 50kg bomb was filled with 20kg (44lbs) of explosive, the 100kg bomb with 47.75kg (103lbs), the 250kg bomb with 104kg (230lbs), and the 500kg bomb 223kg (491lbs). The steel casing and fins made up the balance of the weight.

The 50kg bomb was effective against troops in the open and aircraft on the ground, especially single-engine aircraft. The 100kg bomb could destroy a multi-engine transport, and potentially destroy or damage several. The larger bombs were more effective against buildings than parked aircraft due to their size. The blast radius was not significantly bigger than that of a 100kg bomb, and fewer could be carried. The 250kg bomb could take down the lightly constructed wood frame buildings typically used at Allied airfields for maintenance shops, hangars, or warehouses. The 500kg bomb could bring down a reinforced building. A direct hit by either would destroy a fuel or ammunition dump, even if stored in a bunker.

When the Pacific War started the IJN Air Force was using tactics employed during the Second Sino-Japanese War, which began in 1937. That is to say they were using the aerial tactics of the Great War. Even their organization reflected this. The *chutai* (or squadrons) were made up of three flights of three aircraft (with three reserve aircraft filling in when aircraft were out of service). They flew in tight vics of three aircraft. Each had an officer or senior NCO leading, a junior NCO in the second slot, and a trainee pilot in the third slot. In fighter units, the three aircraft operated together in a tight formation, until combat occurred.

Combat featured individual dogfights. Maneuverability was emphasized, almost exaggeratedly so. Pilots favored maneuverability over speed. IJA pilots disliked the retractable landing gear of the Hayabusa because it added weight and reduced maneuverability. These tactics worked well against Chinese pilots of the Second Sino-Japanese War and well enough in the initial phases of the Pacific War, when IJA pilots were engaging second-rate Allied aircraft in the opening months of the invasion of Burma.

Allied hit-and-run tactics avoided dogfighting. They used the Allied aircrafts' superior diving speed and rugged

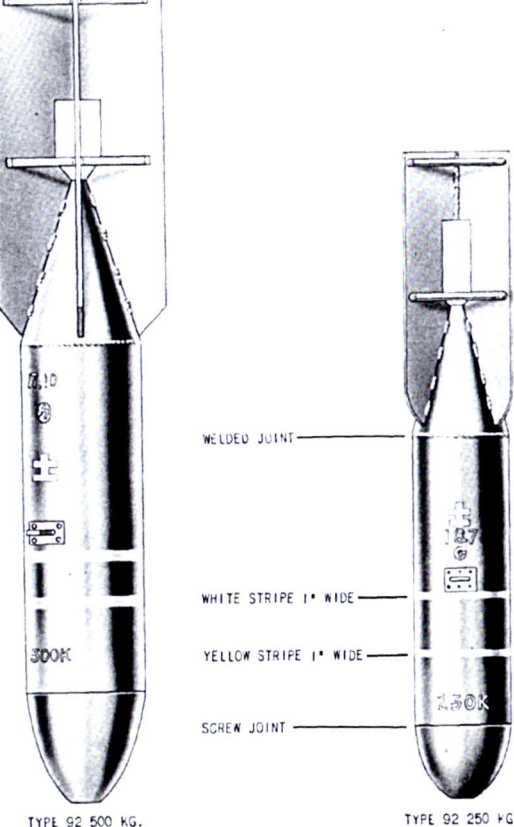

The heaviest bombs used by the Japanese against the Assam airfields were Type 92 500kg and 250kg high-explosive bombs shown here. The Imperial Japanese Army also used 50kg and 100kg bombs. The 500kg bomb would have been used against buildings, while the 250kg bomb was used to crater runways. (AC)

construction to make one pass at an enemy aircraft, escape, then return for a second pass. It made traditional IJA tactics obsolete. First employed by the American Volunteer Group in Burma, it played to Allied strengths and Japanese weaknesses in aircraft design.

The IJA Air Force evolved to use the *schwarm* tactics employed initially by the Luftwaffe, and eventually by Allied air forces. The vic was replaced by the finger four, a loose formation made up of two pairs of two aircraft, with a lead and wingman in each pair, and one pair covering a lead pair. This deemphasized pure maneuverability, but better used the superior speed of retractable-gear, closed-cockpit aircraft.

When Japanese fighters encountered unarmed transports, conventional aerial combat tactics were abandoned. Due to transports' lack of defensive armament and the light armament of Japanese fighters, the best approach to take was closing to the minimum distance possible and firing at ranges so close the fighter could not miss. The transports' engines were the most rewarding target. Knocking out even one engine made it difficult for the transport to maintain altitude or even keep flying.

This required finding transports. There was a lot of space between Assam and China. A fighter was unlikely to encounter a transport in a random search. The Japanese in Upper Burma lacked radar with which to spot US transports and a ground control system to vector their fighters to intercept them. An encounter was random chance. Even in Hump southern routes within range of Japanese fighters, an encounter was so unlikely that this route was safer than the high mountains of the northern routes.

The Japanese occasionally sent squadron sweeps hunting transports, but this burned too much fuel to justify the losses incurred by transports. Normally, only single-fighter (or a fighter and wingman) patrols were conducted. Their main value was herding aircraft north, where the weather and mountains took a bigger toll than Japanese fighters.

Japan occasionally bombed and strafed the Assam airfields. The bombers attacked in tight vics of three, with fighters escorting them to protect the bombers from Allied fighters. Against aircraft in revetments (when they existed), 50kg bombs were most effective due to the number that could be carried. Against buildings, 250kg bombs were preferred. Strafing yielded few results. The single 7.7mm machine guns of the bombers or twin 7.7mm or 12.7mm machine guns of the fighters were too light to do much damage.

When the Japanese launched raids against the Assam airfields, the bombers flew in tight formations in groups of three, similar to the formation the Ki-21 bombers are flying in this picture. Fighters began the war fighting in vee formation, emphasizing dogfighting, but switched to the looser four-finger formation by 1943. (Wikipedia)

CAMPAIGN OBJECTIVES
Keeping China in the war

While the campaign objectives of both the Japanese and Allies differed, both had similar sets of goals and objectives. The most important similarity was that for both, except Great Britain which originally possessed it, the occupation of Burma was secondary. Burma was the means to an end – controlling the supply line to China.

That made it an accidental campaign, unexpected by both sides. Japan believed it achieved its goals once it occupied enough of Burma to cut the Burma Road. The airlift started by the US was unanticipated by Japan, especially after it occupied Myitkyina. Japan believed holding Myitkyina eliminated the ability to fly supplies to China. Suddenly it had a new challenge to achieve its objective.

The US had not planned a major airlift to China at the campaign's outset, not at the scale it quickly grew to. They had unexpected challenges building the infrastructure to support the airlift and providing aircraft to conduct it. The goals kept shifting as the war progressed.

A second similarity was that, for both sides, what the US called the China-Burma-India Theater (Burma and Chinese and Indian provinces adjacent to it) held low priority. Every other theater of war was more important. For both Japan and the Allies, Burma and the CBI got what was left over. For both sides, it was located at the far end of the world. Supplies had to move a minimum of 10,000 miles to reach the theater from the United States and up to 13,000 miles early in the war. For Japan the trip was at least 3,000 miles, shorter than the Allies, but no less formidable given Japan's more limited resources.

Finally, and paradoxically given there was a land route from India to China, it was primarily an aerial campaign. Jungles, mountains, and absence of roads and railroads made Upper Burma, where the campaign largely took place, impenetrable by land, except on foot. Initially supplies could only reach China by air. Even later, when the Ledo Road was completed and the Burma Road reopened, it was easier to fly supplies to China than to drive them there. Aerial resupply was the easiest way to support troops in this theater.

Both sides had to plan a campaign where aircraft, not armies, dictated campaign goals and objectives. It was hitherto unexplored territory, rewarding flexibility and initiative.

Roosevelt thought US aid would keep China in the war and help transform it into a western-style liberal republic. Although most of the supplies carried supported US forces in China, donations to China included transport aircraft like this C-47 flown and operated by CNAC, the Chinese national airline. (NMAF)

OPPOSITE THE SUPPLY LINE

The China airlift led to an unanticipated campaign with unexpected challenges and benefits. Not only were tonnages ultimately carried far beyond expectations, so were some of the cargoes. By the end there were mass movements of Chinese troops, with tens of thousands of men moved by air. (AC)

Allied objectives and plans

The China airlift's objective was keeping China in the war. Even before the Pacific phase of World War II opened, Britain and the US supported China in its struggles against Japan. Britain helped created the Burma Road, running from Lashio, Burma to Kunming in China's adjacent Yunnan Province. The US supplied China with munitions, even fostering the American Volunteer Group.

Once Japan opened hostilities against the US and Britain, keeping China in the war grew more critical. The ongoing war in China tied down the Imperial Japanese Army. Western war planners feared a separate peace by China with Japan would free hundreds of thousands of IJA soldiers to face US, British, and Commonwealth forces.

In 1942 China was the closest Allied-held territory to Japan. To US war planners, China seemed the quickest route to Tokyo. From Chinese-held territory, Japan's Home Islands were within range of the soon-to-be-operational B-29 super-heavy bombers. If China's army could be reequipped, retrained, and reorganized, it could regain enough territory to bring Japan within range of existing B-17 and B-24 bombers. If China retook its coast, the US could use its ports to invade Japan, just 500 miles away.

On paper it seemed achievable. China had the world's largest population. The US could provide enough weapons to equip an overwhelming Chinese Army from China's population, if means could be found to get them there. Planners thought it possible the US war economy would produce enough munitions to make it possible to reequip the entire Chinese Army by 1945.

President Roosevelt also saw US assistance as a means to transform China into a representative republic along classical liberal lines. China's Kuomintang, desperate for aid, encouraged Roosevelt's belief. Publicity savvy, Kuomintang made sure the US viewed the Kuomintang government as the political inheritors of Sun Yat-sen who established China as

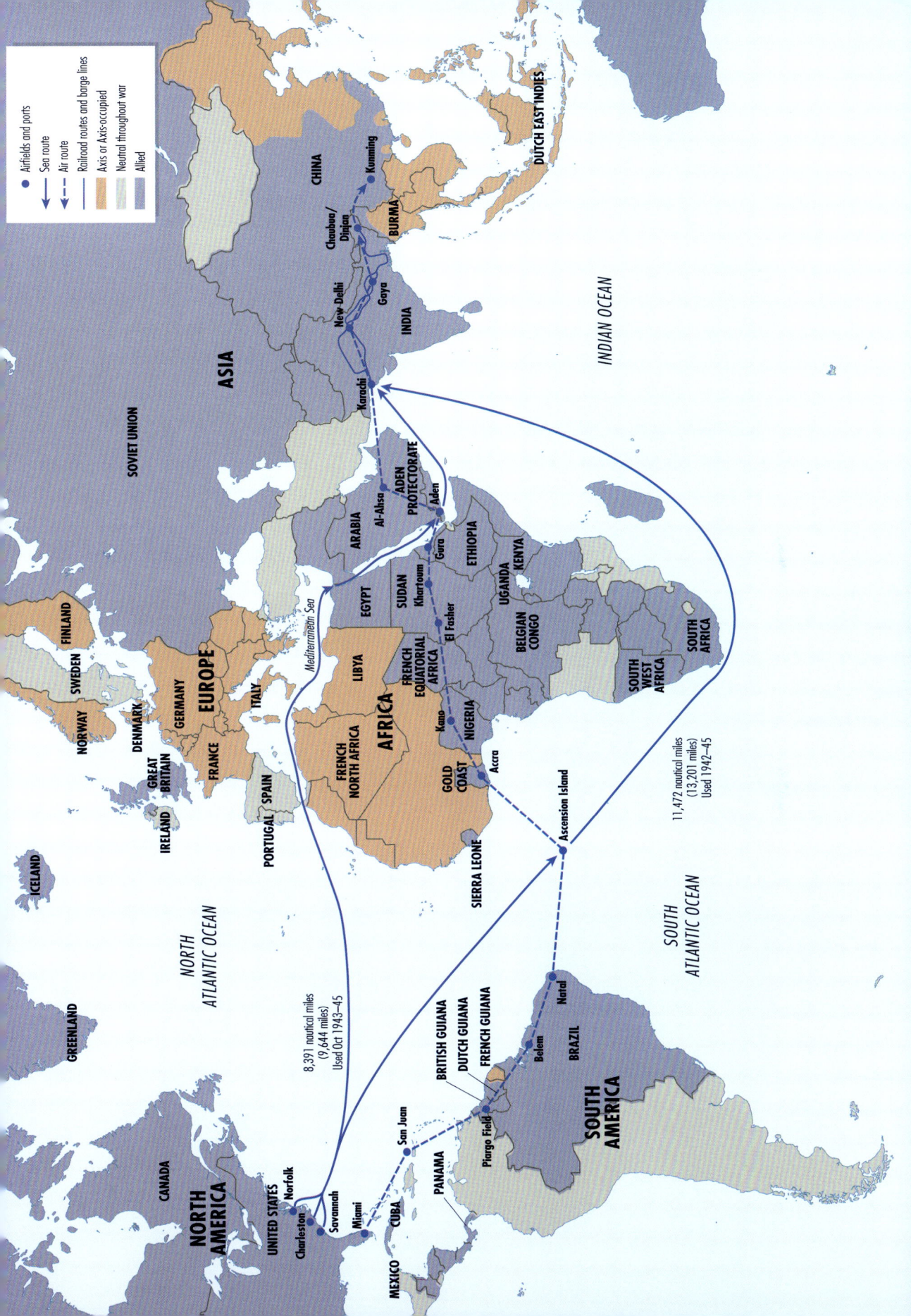

a republic along Western lines in 1911. Roosevelt saw a republican China as a major Asian power to serve as an American ally in the postwar world.

The question was *how* to get US resources to China. The Burma Road was closing in the early months of 1942. No remaining overland route to China existed. In January 1942 T. V. Soong offered another option – flying supplies to China from India. He proposed an airlift of 12,000 tons of supplies per month. He calculated it would take 100 C-47 or C-53 transports each flying two tons of supplies 60 trips per month.

China offered 35 CNAC C-53s from domestic airline routes for the India-China airlift. The US need only provide 65 more transports. Roosevelt, never overly concerned with technical details, thought the proposal worthwhile. He directed General Henry "Hap" Arnold to investigate its feasibility. If Arnold could not start it immediately, he was to report the best way to start an airlift with the resources available.

On February 2, 1942, the War Department assessed possible air routes to China. They decided it could be done by flying from Assam to a newly completed airfield at Myitkyina, Burma. Cargoes would be loaded onto barges and taken to Bhamo, then driven to Kunming along the Burma Road.

This plan ignored practical reality. Combat in Burma meant transports would be flying through an active war zone. Well before the airlift started, Myitkyina fell to Japan, nullifying the original plan. But the airlift to China was gaining momentum.

The concept of an "aerial Burma Road" was too compelling to abandon. Plans and resources to create it were already in motion. From the start, the airlift was as much symbolic as strategic. While the supplies taken to China were ill-defined, one purpose was not. The airlift was viewed as one of the most effective ways of encouraging China, of providing evidence of US friendship towards and support of China. Simply doing it was seen as just as important as the reason for doing it.

Even before deciding how many tons of cargo and what to send (and why), resources streamed to Assam. The British built airfields for the Americans. The US sent transports and personnel to India. They created an organization infrastructure in the form of a dedicated air force, the Tenth, to support airlift operations. Only a plan was missing.

That plan came together by the end of 1942. Arnold intended to send 75 Douglas transports, C-47s or C-53s to Assam starting March 1942. Once there, they were expected to fly 7,500 tons of supplies per month to China. This required 100 flights per day, with a round trip flight time of six hours. Assuming the 35 promised CNAC C-53s appeared, it required virtually every transport to make one round trip every day.

This was unachievable. There were too few airfields in March to operate 110 twin-engine transports. The plan was scaled back, in tonnage and number of aircraft until infrastructure could be built. That did not matter. By July the goal was carrying 7,500 tons of cargo per month by December 1942 and thereafter. There was no real plan through most of 1942, just an ad hoc collection of aircraft, cargoes, and flights. It was enough the airlift was "keeping China in the war."

Pledged tonnage kept increasing, despite US airlift capabilities or local realities. In May at the Trident Conference, US commanders in China, Joseph Stilwell on

The Cairo Conference, held in November 1943, was the only major summit meeting which Chiang Kai Shek attended. While there he repeated a demand originally made in 1942 for 5,000 tons of supplies delivered to China each month. Roosevelt promised 10,000 tons per month by the end of 1943. (Wikipedia)

the ground and Claire Chennault in the air, wanted the airlift expanded. Stilwell asked for enough supplies to outfit 20 Chinese divisions. Chennault wanted 450 to 500 warplanes operating out of China and the fuel, munitions, and spare parts to support them.

Allied leaders, concerned China would leave the war, decided to deliver 7,000 tons of supplies per month by July, increasing it to 10,000 tons by September. Also agreed was a plan to immediately expand the Assam airfields to support enough aircraft to carry 20,000 tons per month. Even if immediately unavailable, aircraft could be added quicker than airfields expanded. At the Cairo Conference in November 1943, which Chiang attended, he repeated a demand he made in June 1942, for the US to send China 500 aircraft and deliver 5,000 tons of military supplies each month. He was promised 10,000 tons by December.

Throughout the airlift there were three major nations involved, the US, Britain, and China, each with different goals and priorities. Britain's strategic goals in the theater were protecting India from Japanese invasion and regaining prewar colonies lost to Japan. China's primary goal was to survive until the US defeated Japan. The US's primary goal was to use China to tie up Japanese forces to relieve pressure on the US and the Commonwealth Nations in the Pacific. These goals were sometimes mutually exclusive.

Chiang Kai-Shek, advised by his American-educated wife and her brother (T. V. Soong), believed the US entry into the Pacific War doomed Japan. He wanted to husband China's and especially the Kuomintang's military resources until Japan lost. He was looking ahead to a postwar fight with the Chinese Communists for control of China.

He wanted to build up the Nationalist Chinese Army for that struggle using whatever US aid was provided. (Initially the US offered to arm, equip, and train the entire Chinese Army. The size of that commitment caused it to be revised downward, to arming, equipping, and training Chinese Army units supporting US forces in Burma.) Chiang had no intention of (as he saw it) wasting US-trained Chinese troops fighting the Japanese. He needed them postwar.

This was why Chiang made unreasonable demands for troops and supplies, warning China would collapse if those demands went unmet. He did not believe he would get everything

The Ledo Road was started in 1943 to connect with the old Burma Road once the Allies retook Upper Burma. Completed in late 1944 it finally opened in January 1945. This sign at its zero mile marker notes the distances to the various stops on the way. (AC)

he asked for. He believed he would get more than he would by being reasonable. It allowed him to better prepare for the postwar struggle he expected to fight. It generally worked. The Allies went along with his demands, setting unrealistically high delivery quotas early in the war, increasing them as the war progressed. Not until mid-1944, when it was clear the road to Japan went west across the Pacific, not east from China, could the US ignore Chiang. By then the airlift was in place and running well. Inertia kept it running and growing.

Britain had no objection to the US using British India as the staging field for a China airlift. It cost the British little other than space. They had plenty. It also brought more US resources to Assam and Burma, not all of which was devoted to the airlift. The US brought troops and warplanes to protect their bases and engineers to build infrastructure. The US (and US-trained Chinese troops flown to India and Burma for training) also supported an offensive in Upper Burma to reopen the Burma Road and simplify the air route to China.

Britain's main interest was retaking territories taken from it by Japan. Roosevelt did not support reestablishment of colonial empires, French, Dutch, or English. Once the US controlled the parts of Burma needed to support the airlift and reopen the Burma Road, they were done, unwilling to use resources to further (as the US saw it) Britain's colonial ambitions. The US saw a Lower Burma offensive not as liberation of the Burmese people, but as a re-conquest by a colonial power. This led to a divergence of interest between the US and Britain when Britain launched an offensive into Lower Burma. The US would not oppose it, but did not support it, even as it pushed Japan still further from the Hump air routes.

Japanese objectives and plans

Japan's objective in occupying Burma was simple: complete the isolation of China. By December 1941, when the Pacific War started, the Burma Road was China's last link to the outside world. With the fall of Hong Kong, even the CNAC flights outside China were cut off. In many ways, the Burma Road was more symbolic than substantive. Very little could move on it. Regardless, it was there, allowing supplies to flow to China.

After Japan entered Burma in January 1942, the Burma Road became untenable. Ships unloading in Rangoon were subject to air attack. With the occupation of Rangoon in March, the Burma Road's southern terminus was cut. Japan then marched up Burma until it held the railroads feeding the Burma Road. Japan soon occupied all of the Shan State, reaching Lashio, the start of the road portion of the Burma Road.

When Britain started building an airfield at Myitkyina, Japan moved further north and east, taking Upper Burma as far north as Myitkyina and parts of far Western China east of Lashio. The Japanese were unaware that Myitkyina was intended as part of an aerial route to China. Rather, they did not want an enemy airfield threatening their hold on Upper Burma. Regardless, it furthered their goal of isolating China.

In June 1942, Japan halted its advance. It held most of Burma within convenient reach of a railhead or river port. Far north, Kachin State (including Fort Hertz) and a few scraps of Northern Sagaing State were still in British hands, but they hardly mattered. What the British held was rugged mountain and dense jungle, impenetrable by land to organized army formations. Any British advance from that direction would be glacially slow; an army would have to build roads as it advanced.

Japan believed the campaign was over with Japan achieving its main objective. China was isolated. They drew down forces in Burma, especially their air forces. They withdrew the *sentai* equipped with older aircraft to refit them with newer models. Left in Burma were one fighter *sentai*, equipped with Ki-43s and four bomber *sentai* with Ki-51 and K-48 bombers. Even these largely stood down from April to September, the wet monsoon season, to recuperate from the strains of their conquest of Burma. They could afford to. The Allied air forces, British, US, and Chinese, had been driven from Burma.

Rangoon was bombed as early as December 1941, as the Japanese knew it was the starting point for supplies traveling the Burma Road. Japan's main motivation in attacking Burma was cutting the Burma Road, China's last link with the outside world. The Japanese little dreamed an airlift was possible. (Wikipedia)

At first they were unaware the US was attempting to supply China by air. There were only a few flights in April, and a few hundred tons shifted in May 1942. In June the airlift virtually ceased as almost all transports were shifted to dropping supplies to retreating Allied forces in Upper Burma or evacuating soldiers and civilians from Myitkyina. It took until July before Japan finally noticed a new aerial road to China opening.

Japan was slow to react, even then. Initially the airlift seemed unimportant. Japan felt the US simply could not fly enough cargo to China to do more than provide symbolic aid. May marked the beginning of the monsoon rains in Assam and Burma. Torrential rains fell, making air operations – for both sides – extremely difficult. The Imperial Japanese Army was willing to let the US risk their aircraft in the monsoon rains unmolested by Japan.

The Japanese moved their aircraft south to airfields near Mandalay and Rangoon to wait out the monsoon. Myitkyina airfield went unused through the summer of 1942. Operations in Upper Burma were discontinued until the rains stopped. Japan permitted the airlift to operate unmolested until Japanese-held Upper Burma airfields dried out in September, after the monsoon rains ceased. The IJA Air Force in Burma was reinforced by two *sentai* of Ki-43s by then as the *sentai* withdrawn in March to upgrade from Ki-27s returned.

Even after August 1942, the Japanese response in Burma was halfhearted and unfocused. They launched a few bombing and strafing raids on the Assam airfields from which the airlift originated in October, but that was it. Doing this required the aircraft to arm up and launch from Lower Burma, stage to Myitkyina where they refueled and fly to the Assam airfields, which they would bomb.

Attacking airfields served Japan better than attempting to intercept transports while flying airlift. There were few Japanese fighters, and in 1942 relatively few transports were in the air at any one time. The maximum effort during that period would have been a few-dozen flights per day. The odds of finding one of three to four transports scattered over a 500-plus-mile route each hour using only the fighter pilots' eyesight was astronomically low. The Japanese did not bother. It was not worth the fuel burned.

Given the Japanese scarcity of aircraft, especially fighters, their limited response was understandable. Through the end of 1942, Japan's assessment that the airlift was symbolic

Japan withdrew most of its fighter *sentais* from Burma after capturing Myitkyina. This allowed those units to replace obsolete Ki-27s with more modern Ki-43s. Too many Ki-27s, like this one, were being shot down in combat. This left the Japanese short of fighters in Burma until the monsoon ended. (AC)

seemed correct. The Tenth Air Force was flying very little to Kunming, through most of that period. They were flying only a few hundred tons of supplies each month rather than the pledged 5,000 tons. Not until December 1942 did the US top 1,000 tons in one month, flying 1,227 tons.

Japan reassessed this conclusion as 1943 continued. By April the Allies were flying thousands of tons per month. Over the summer, the flight rate increased from 3,000 tons to 5,000 tons. Japan realized the US had reopened a significant supply line with China which needed to be closed. The IJA Air Force commanders in Burma began to take the airlift seriously. The problem was how to respond. As in 1942 they had to wait out the monsoon months before they could execute new plans against the airlift.

As an interim measure, in June they started a sabotage campaign at the Chinese airlift airfields at Yunnanyi and Kunming. The agent hired to lead the effort was caught in Chungking, before he could do anything substantive, and was shot. They also installed false homing beacons in north Burma to lure transports off course. These apparently had little effect because in 1943 the real homing beacons were so unreliable US pilots rarely trusted them.

When the weather cleared in October, Japan launched two efforts against the US in an effort to gain air superiority over the airlift route. There were a series of air raids on the Assam airfields that continued off and on from October 1943 to March 1944. It lacked sufficient resources to be effective and was discontinued when the 1944 monsoon began in April.

Japan also launched Operation *Tsuzigiri* ("Street Murder") in October. This was an attempt to interdict the airlift with fighter patrols across the Hump routes. By then, flight density had increased enough to make it worthwhile. Flights of four to eight aircraft were sent to attack transports as they crossed Burma. It was initially successful due to surprise, but US countermeasures nullified the effort and it was discontinued after three weeks.

The Japanese also attempted to interdict the airlift using ground troops. In 1942 and 1943, the Japanese moved further north into Burma, both to take territory in which to set up their false homing beacons and to deprive the US of locations used by forward observation posts used to provide early warning of Japanese air raids against the Assam airfields.

Since Japan could not stop the airlift with their air assets, in spring 1944 it attempted to do so with their army. They launched a ground offensive against Manipur, east of Assam. The goal was to sever the railroad and barge lines feeding the airlift airfields with supplies.

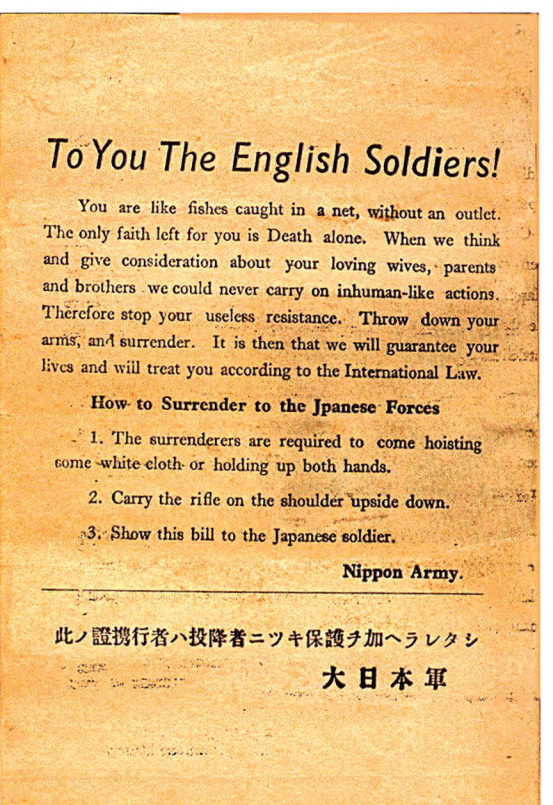

It required crossing a roadless jungle with an army using infiltration tactics. (Ironically, this was inspired by the British Chindit groups which perfected jungle infiltration tactics. The Chindits thought they were emulating the Japanese. In turn, the Japanese concluded that if the British could successfully use large-scale infiltration that meant Japan could too.)

The plan had the virtue of providing a decisive solution to killing the airlift. Its shortcomings only became apparent once it was executed. Japan successfully infiltrated, but lacked the heavy weapons necessary to take fortified towns. Ultimately it fell short, failing to reach the railroad.

With the failure of that offensive, Japan lost the ability to interfere with the airlift. A combination of growing Allied air power, an influx of Allied ground forces (including Chinese units), and the Allied ability to resupply its ground forces in Burma by air allowed the Allied forces to launch a land offensive in Upper Burma. By October, the Allies held Myitkyina and its airfield. They built a second airfield for its tactical aircraft, and quickly established air superiority over Upper Burma. By January 1945, the IJA Air Force had to evacuate Mandalay, and by March, its aircraft could only operate from airfields in Burma's southern panhandle. That left the IJA too far away from the Hump air routes to attack them, even when they shifted south, stopping at Myitkyina before heading to China.

The Japanese invasion of India was a last, desperate attempt to stop the airlift. It culminated well short of its goals. The Japanese tried to bluff British and Commonwealth forces into surrendering, using techniques like leaflet drops. Their previous treatment of prisoners left Allied forces unconvinced of the promises made. (AC)

THE CAMPAIGN
Stopping the airlift

A C-46 flies over the Lower Himalayas as it flies between India and China. The towering peaks aircraft had to cross to reach China from India gave the passage "the Hump" as a nickname. Pilots felt as if they were flying over the roof of the world. (NMAF)

The China airlift was one of the most unique campaigns of World War II. It was one of the longest, stretching from March 1942 to August 1945. Perhaps only the Battle of the Atlantic was longer. It was an ongoing, single campaign with a single objective throughout: supplying China. It was also unique in that it was primarily a logistics effort, involving very little actual fighting. The side that instigated it actually wanted to avoid combat, or at least minimize it.

If the defender is defined as the side wishing to prevent something, the Japanese were the defenders in this campaign. Like the defender in a football game (American or European), they were trying to prevent the US from achieving its goal of supplying China by air. Every ton of cargo carried to China was a point scored by the US. The only way for the Japanese to stop the airlift was to go on the attack. They had to destroy the airfields used or the aircraft carrying the supplies. This was another unique aspect of the campaign.

It was also a campaign defined by logistics and infrastructure. Both sides had to bring things long distances simply to conduct activities. "Get there first with the most" was key to victory, but in this case what you had to get there first with was not really traditional military formations. It was the supplies and resources to maintain those formations and to provide the bases to support them. Both sides had to build airports and roads before they could fight.

The US was constrained as to what it could bring to China by the available infrastructure. The Japanese attempts to stop the airlift were constrained by the supplies they had available for their forces. Mastery of the theater followed mastery of logistics.

It was also a campaign of technological contrasts. Some of what were then mankind's most technologically advanced machines co-existed with some of the most primitive societies around. Complex transports were loaded by beasts of burden or ended up carrying draft animals as priority cargoes. Twentieth-century men worked alongside those using thousand-year-old technology.

It was a campaign defined by geography. Terrain and weather frequently proved more ferocious obstacles than the enemy's forces – for both sides. The mountains and jungles in and around Burma were among the most forbidding terrain in the world to ground forces attempting to move through them. The weather was equally challenging in the air. Warm humid air from the tropical oceans collided with frigid mountain air.

The resulting collision yielded the worst flying weather in the world. Aircraft would lift off 130°F runways with 95 percent humidity to plunge into frigid temperatures two to five miles up. They routinely encountered fog, severe icing, and storm-force winds with every trip across the mountains between India and China. The trip took them across high mountains – among the world's highest terrain. Those that traveled it called it "the Hump." It demonstrated the capability of air power to project force, and maintain armies in ways previously undreamed of.

Supplying China: July 1937 to March 1942

China dominated Asia from the 1300s to the late 1700s. Neighbors, including Japan, paid homage. The appearance of European seafarers in the 1600s coincided with a period of Chinese internal decay. By the late 1800s China's Imperial government was moribund; its power in eclipse.

In the 1850s, Japan, previously a hermit kingdom broken into factions, reentered the world. It reunited. Adopting European technology, the country industrialized, building armies and navies along European lines. The power vacuum caused by China's collapse was filled by Japan. The 1904–05 Russo-Japanese War, when Japan defeated a European power, raised the country to even greater prominence.

China's imperial government collapsed in 1911, replaced by a republic in 1912 led by the Kuomintang (KMT). When Yuan Shikai, the first elected president of the republic, declared himself emperor, years of civil war followed. The Chinese Communist Party (CCP) emerged in 1927 with help from the Soviet Union. Chiang Kai-Shek, by then head of the Kuomintang, reunited China under the KMT with CCP help. Chiang moved the Chinese capital to Nanking. Having subdued the warlords, Chiang kicked out the Soviets and purged the CCP. The Communists were pushed into China's remote northern interior.

Although Chiang now ruled all China, it was an unsteady, restive rule. Both the Communists and regional warlords sought to regain power. In July 1937 Japan invaded China, the third war Japan had fought with China since the 1890s. The first two, the First Sino-Japanese War

Nanking was the Kuomintang capital in 1937. Shown here under attack by Japanese forces, it was captured in December 1937. The Imperial Japanese Army expected the Chinese to surrender after the loss of their capital. Instead Chiang relocated China's capital to Wuhan and refused to surrender. (USNHHC)

(1894–95) and the Mukden Incident (1931), had been short, victorious wars for Japan, yielding quick territorial gains at China's expense. Japan expected no less this time around.

Japan made many gains in the war's first year. In August Japanese troops took Shanghai, China's most important port. They took the Kuomintang capital, Nanking, in December. By January 1938, China's organized military was largely defeated. Japan paused, awaiting a Chinese surrender. Instead, the Kuomintang government refused to surrender. Chiang moved the capital to Wuhan, and concentrated on rebuilding his armed forces. He was supported, even if passively or tacitly, by China's population.

Many Chinese hated Chiang and his government. A republic in name only, it was a dictatorship Chiang ran for his benefit. The Chinese, including the remaining warlords, hated the Japanese more. Japanese troops behaved barbarically during the war. Atrocities such as the Rape of Nanking hardened Chinese resolve. Even the Communists preferred Chiang to the Japanese. Willing to play the long game, they were content to let the Kuomintang and Japanese fight in hopes they would exhaust each other.

The Imperial Japanese Army responded by pushing deeper into China. Japan launched a new offensive to surround and destroy the new troops Chiang had raised. Japan captured Wuhan in October. Again, instead of surrendering, Chiang and the Kuomintang government retreated, relocating their capital to Chungking. The war continued.

Japan was faced with the prospect of endless war. They started a war they could not end. Japan lacked the manpower to occupy all of China. Japan could take any territory it chose, but that required troops from the garrisons in territories they previously held. Unoccupied or lightly garrisoned regions reverted to Kuomintang or Communist control.

During their 1938 advances, Japan moved into regions occupied by the remnants of the CCP, which had been rebuilding. Mao's forces were as willing to ambush Japanese troops as they were to attack Kuomintang forces. Japan faced an insurgency in those areas, which tied down more Japanese forces. It slowly dawned on the Japanese government and IJA they were riding a Chinese dragon they could not get off without a humiliating withdrawal or a Kuomintang surrender.

Japan was unwilling to withdraw from captured territory. Japan knew China needed imported munitions to continue fighting. China needed imports for its people to survive. Japan controlled China's best industrial areas and agricultural land. Japan initiated a new strategy to defeat China. Isolate China from the world. Wait for a lack of munitions to debilitate Free China's armies and starvation to weaken its people.

Japan began cutting China off from the outside world. It started by invading China's principal remaining ports. Using the Imperial Navy to lift troops, Japan captured Amoy in May 1938 and nearby Foochow a few weeks later. They landed at Swatow in June, carving out an enclave around the port.

In December 1938 Japan launched a massive invasion of coastal China around Canton. Since the then-neutral British Crown Colony of Hong Kong was close to Canton, they took a much larger swath of coastal China around Canton than they had in their previous landings. This sealed off Hong Kong from Free China, making it virtually impossible to run cargoes into China.

Finally in February 1939, Japan occupied Hainan. The island was not a port, but its occupation allowed Japan to monitor the French concession in China, the port of Luichow. Prize rules allowed them to stop and search ships in Chinese territorial waters, making it more difficult to use Luichow to run supplies to Kuomintang-controlled Free China. Hainan's capture stopped the flow of cargo to Chinese ports, but not to China. Three routes remained open.

The first was a sea route. It started at Haiphong, a northern harbor in then-neutral French Indochina. France was sympathetic to China. From Haiphong, munitions traveled to Hanoi, the French Indochina terminus of a railroad running into Free China. This was China's principal supply route for nearly a year.

The second route circumventing the Japanese blockade was along the old Silk Road, running overland out of China to Europe. By the 20th century, it was passable by motor vehicles, but was impractical for anything but the lightest cargoes. Trucks needed cached fuel, and the route was extremely rough. Plus its major western terminus was in the Soviet Union, which had other matters to attend to after the German invasion of Russia in 1941. It closed in early 1942.

Finally there was the Burma Road. It was the newest route. Chiang started the project shortly after the Second Sino-Japanese War started. It finally opened for traffic in November 1939. The road ran from Kunming to Lashio. Supplies arrived at Rangoon, and were carried by rail to Lashio. From there they were trucked into China along a winding road with steep grades that wound through mountains and over deep river gorges. The trip took a minimum of ten days.

It was a low-volume route. It carried more than the Silk Road, but Rangoon could only handle 40,000 tons of cargo monthly. The Burma Road's carrying capacity was even lower. While open it never carried more than 3,000 tons per month. (One World War II-era US infantry division consumed 6,000 tons of supplies per month.) The major supply route ran through Haiphong. A single moderate-sized freighter carried 5,000 tons, and a single train moved 2,100 to 3,500 tons of cargo to China.

For 14 months, from February 1939 through to May 1940, all the Japanese could do was watch as trains carrying tens of thousands of tons per month unloaded at Haiphong for onward transportation to China. France was too strong to challenge, even after World War II in Europe began in September 1939. Then, between April and June 1940, Germany launched a series of lightning offensives including one conquering France.

Before June ended, Japan demanded France close supply routes to China through Haiphong and Luichow, allow Japanese inspectors into Haiphong to monitor compliance, and permit Japanese naval vessels to operate from Luichow. France successfully refused

Unable to force the Kuomintang to surrender, the Japanese attempted to starve China out by isolating it from the rest of the world. In 1938 Japan captured most of the Kuomintang-controlled ports in China, including Canton. Its largest southern port, it is shown here under air attack. (USNHHC)

Hump flight profiles

Terrain, weather, and an aircraft's capabilities combined to dictate the flight paths used in the China airlift. Some aircraft types could master the soaring heights of the Hump, others could not. Some handled icing well; others had to totally avoid ice. This dictated the flight profiles used by different aircraft.

Key: US flights

A. C-47: Route typically flown during 1942 or 1943, direct to Kunming over lower terrain.
B. C-87: Route typically flown during 1943 or 1944, the official route, flying over icing conditions.
C. C-46: Route typically flown during 1943 or 1944, the official route, flying through icing conditions.
D. C-54: Route typically flown during 1944 or 1945, from Bengal to Kunming over low mountains.

EVENTS

1. Aircraft takes off.
2. Aircraft crosses Naga Hills or Arkan Mountains.
3. Aircraft over Burma.
4. Aircraft crosses Lower Himalayas or Shan Hills.
5. Aircraft lands.

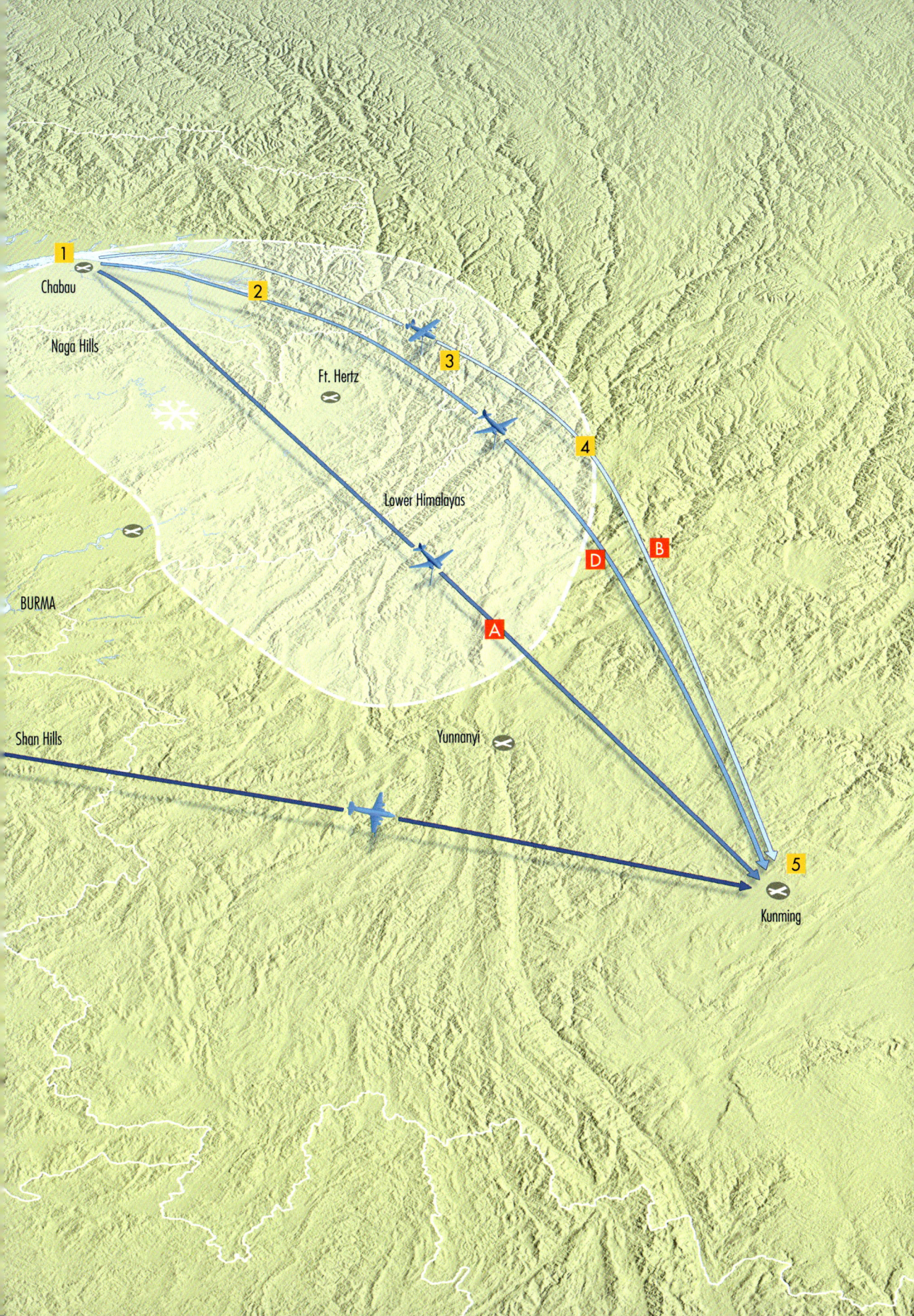

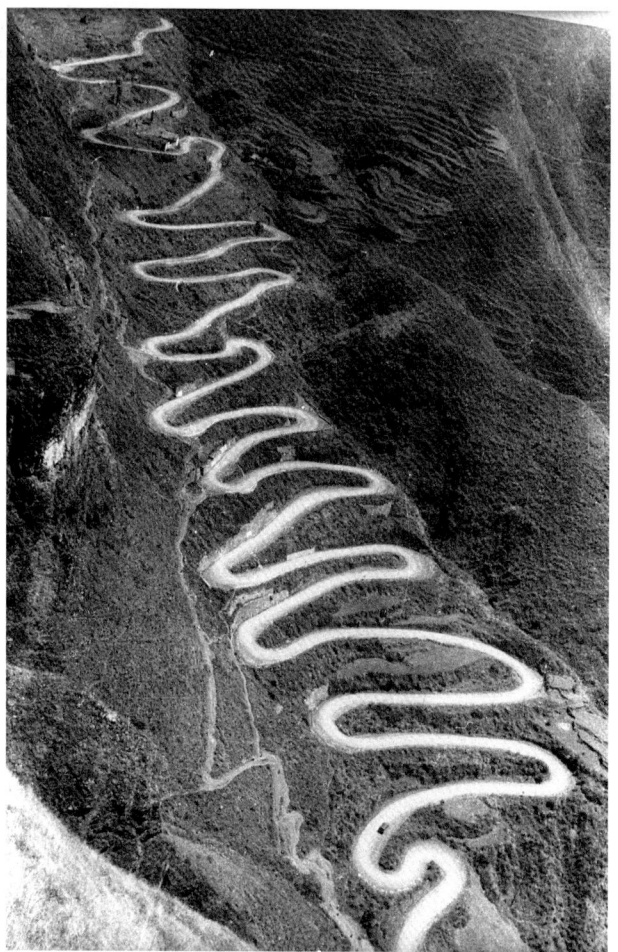

After Haiphong was closed in June 1940, China's sole remaining link to the outside world was the Burma Road. Running from Lashio to Kunming, its road distance was nearly twice the direct distance due to the many switchbacks needed to negotiate the mountainous terrain it passed through. (NMAF)

to permit inspectors or granting ship basing rights, but agreed to shut both ports to China traffic. In July 1940 Japan demanded Britain close the Burma Road. Fighting alone for its survival, anticipating an attempted German invasion, and not wishing further complications with Japan, Britain complied.

China was now isolated. Had Japan been content with that, China would likely have been starved into submission by 1943. Yet Japan pushed things further. In September it signed the Tripartite Pact, joining a military alliance with Germany and Italy. France was not a signatory to the alliance. It had split into a "Free French" government-in-exile still allied with Britain, and a Vichy French government subservient to Germany. Vichy ran French Indochina. Once Japan joined the Axis, the IJA occupied Tonkin, Indochina's northernmost province.

It was unauthorized. Japan's government apologized, and withdrew. It then "negotiated" a treaty with the French colonial government to permit Japan to occupy Tonkin with 6,000 troops, base warships in Luichow, and allow Japan to operate warplanes at three airfields in Tonkin. The action outraged both the US and Britain. The US embargoed scrap iron and steel sales to Japan. Britain reopened the Burma Road, breaking China's isolation.

Once the road reopened, the US began supplying China with military aid through it. This included an agreement to send China obsolescent P-40B fighters once destined for Britain. To fly them, volunteers from the US air services were recruited to serve as pilots. The organization, known as the American Volunteer Group, was led by an ex-US Army Air Corps officer, Claire Chennault. He had been serving as air advisor to China since 1937.

This only temporarily deterred Japan. In July 1941 it renegotiated its treaty with France. New terms allowed Japan to occupy all of Indochina with Japanese soldiers and gain the use of five more airfields in Indochina and Cam Ranh Bay as a Japanese naval anchorage. In exchange, France would be permitted to continue the civil administration of the colony.

The agreement alarmed the US, Britain, and the Netherlands, all with possessions close to Indochina. Indochinese bases put Japan in striking distance of these. The US froze Japanese assets in the US and demanded Japan withdraw from Indochina. When Japan ignored the ultimatum, the US embargoed petroleum product sales to Japan. Within a week, Britain and the Netherlands followed suit.

Without imported oil, Japan would grind to a halt. The US assumed this would force Japan to withdraw from Indochina. Instead, Japan decided to go to war in December 1941, and seize British and Dutch oilfields in the Malay Peninsula and the Indonesian Archipelago, something holding Indochina positioned them to do. Japan also attacked US possessions in the Pacific, taking the Philippines, Guam, and Wake Island.

China was tying down most of the Imperial Japanese Army. The other traditional mainland Asian military counterweight to Japan, the Soviet Union, was tied down in an existential struggle with Germany around Moscow, at the far end of the Soviet Union from Siberia. The Burma Road, the last remaining open supply line to China, assumed critical importance. Yet as plans were being laid in London and Washington to improve it, Japan was acting to close it.

Burma was lightly defended when the Pacific War started. British Empire ground forces there were largely constabulary. The air forces there consisted of a few RAF squadrons equipped with third-line obsolescent aircraft and the AVG (the American Volunteer Group, the Flying Tigers), training in Lashio. Burma was assumed to be a rear-echelon backwater, shielded by Malaya and Singapore, where 100,000 British and Commonwealth troops were stationed. Instead, in early January 1942, unprepared for war, it found itself on the front line.

Seeking to close the Burma Road, Japan included Burma in its early expansion plan. Japan bullied Thailand into joining their alliance, offering Thailand parts of the Burmese Shan State as spoils. Japan swept through the Malay Peninsula, trapping most of the enemy troops there in Singapore. (It surrendered on February 15.)

In early January Japan invaded Burma from Thailand with two divisions, with the objective of taking Rangoon. In February they trapped the main Commonwealth force in Burma, a hastily sent Indian division, against the Salween River, destroying two-thirds of it. The British could no longer hold Rangoon. Its port facility and oil refineries were destroyed on March 7. The Japanese entered it the next day.

In the air their only real opposition was the AVG, still in Burma, training. Despite a desperate struggle, the AVG was forced back into China. The AVG inflicted greater losses on the Japanese than it suffered (although not nearly as many as AVG propaganda claimed), but was outnumbered and poorly supplied.

Japan cut the Burma Road by taking Rangoon. Its original war plans anticipated holding only Lower Burma, with no movement north. Rangoon's fall, and its panicked evacuation (thousands of civilians died fleeing on foot through the Burmese jungles to Assam) revealed how weak the British hold on Burma was. The Japanese reinforced Burma with troops available after Singapore fell.

In March and April, Japan swept east to the Indian border and north into Upper Burma. British and Commonwealth forces stopped the westward Japanese advance near the Indian border in May. Two Chinese divisions, led by US General Joseph Stilwell (sent to China in February to coordinate US aid and help train Chinese troops), attempted to stop the

The American Volunteer Group, also known as the Flying Tigers, were ex-US Navy and Army fliers who joined China's air force. Operating outmoded P-40Bs, they provided some of the only effective resistance to the Japanese advance in Burma. The unit was absorbed into the US Army Air Force in mid-1942. (AC)

Japanese moving north. They were flanked and trapped when Thai forces invaded. After briefly attempting to hold Myitkyina, this force disintegrated. Remnants escaped back to India and China, including a party led by Stilwell.

By June, Japan held most of Burma, including all its airfields, and all of the Burma Road within Burma. China was once again isolated.

Opening the air bridge: April 1942 to November 1942

Even before Japan closed the Burma Road, alternative means of supplying China were developing in both China and Washington. As early as January, T. V. Soong proposed resupplying China by air. His proposal was based on a rough calculation that 100 DC-3 equivalents could carry 12,000 tons of cargo each month by air to China. Roosevelt thought this a low-resource operation, since Soong's proposal required a contribution of only 65 C-47s by the United States. General Arnold, handed the job, cut orders sending 75 C-47s to India to support the airlift, starting in March.

Arnold assigned the job to the Tenth Air Force, commanded by Major General Lewis Brereton, then forming in India. Arnold also named Brigadier General Earl Naiden, Brereton's chief of staff, commander of the air transport operation. This gave Naiden two jobs; to simultaneously act as Brereton's executive officer and lead an independent transportation command.

Brereton objected to George C. Marshall, Army Chief of Staff. Brereton was upset an independent command, which he had responsibility to support and protect, was operating within his territory. Arnold had created the split precisely to prevent Brereton from using airlift aircraft for Tenth Air Force missions. Marshall told Brereton that Washington would administer the ferry system, including its aircraft. Essentially Marshall told Brereton to "shut up and soldier."

Upon receiving his assignment, Naiden surveyed the route and the resources available. In March 1942 there were two Assam airfields capable of supporting transports, Chabua

China National Aviation Corporation (CNAC) had years of experience flying in China. Its pilots pioneered the aerial route between China and India. Pan American Airlines owned 40% of CNAC and provided the pilots, some of whom are shown here. USAAF pilots resented the better pay the civilian CNAC pilots received. (NMAF)

and Dinjan. Others could be built, but Naiden believed construction could not start until the monsoon season ended in October. Naiden recommended Arnold send only 25 C-47s until then.

Naiden divided the air transport organization into two commands: the Trans-India Ferry Command and the Assam-Burma Ferry Command. The former managed airlift from Karachi to Assam in India. The Assam-Burma Command (ABC) took cargoes from there to China. Naiden gave Colonel Caleb B. Hayes, originally sent to India to command a B-17 unit in China, command of the ABC. Hayes's deputy was Colonel William Donald Old.

The route Naiden plotted in March involved flying from Dinjan to Myitkyina to Yunnanyi and from there to Kunming. It was a number of short hops, easily flown by even green transport pilots. More importantly, it had only one real high spot; the 10,000ft ridge of mountains between Dinjan and Myitkyina. These were easily surmountable by the C-47 and allowed more cargo to be carried. It was the route plotted by CNAC pilots in 1941.

It also anticipated Japan would stay in Lower Burma – which the Japanese originally planned. They planned to stop at Mandalay. Airfields at Myitkyina and Lashio altered plans. Viewing them as a strategic threat, Japan moved north taking both cities and their airfields. Their task was simplified by Burma's railroad and road network, allowing logistic access to Myitkyina and Lashio. Japan took Lashio in April and Myitkyina in May.

Yet the first flight from India to China bypassed Myitkyina. On April 9 Colonel Old took two C-47s over the 14,000ft-high Kumon Mountains in Burma to Kunming. They carried 1,800 gallons of gasoline intended to refuel the B-25s from the Doolittle Raid,

Hit them at home

At first the Japanese did not realize the US planned to supply China by airlift. When they finally did, the 1942 monsoon season had started and they were withdrawing units from their Burma-based 3rd Hikoshidan to refit with more modern aircraft. They chose to wait for better weather before responding.

In October, the 3rd Hikoshidan launched a series of raids against the four airfields from which transports were flying to China: Dinjan, Chabua, Sookerating, and Mohanbari. The first raid, which targeted Dinjan and Chabua, was the most effective. It achieved surprise, catching the defending fighters on the ground. The antiaircraft defenses of these airfields were rudimentary. As a result, the Japanese could make their attacks virtually unmolested by enemy forces. For the bombers it must have seemed more like a live-fire training exercise than a combat operation.

Of the two airfields hit, Chabua was likely the one hardest hit. It had the only paved runway of the four fields, a strip of macadamized gravel allowing all-weather operations with fully loaded aircraft. It also had the largest contingents of transports of any airfield. Dinjan was where the fighters operated from. That gave the Japanese incentive to hit those two airfields first.

The attack came on October 26, with 54 bombers and 63 fighters sent. (By then the withdrawn fighter *sentai* had completed their transition to Ki-43 and were back in Burma.) The Japanese split their force between Chabua and Dinjan, hitting both simultaneously. They arrived between 1300hrs and 1400hrs local time, early afternoon, with plenty of light to see.

The Ki-21s and Ki-48s worked over the buildings, aircraft, and runways. The Ki-43 split between top cover and strafing parked aircraft. Almost certainly, the Ki-21, with their larger bombloads, concentrated on the buildings, hangars, workshops, and fuel dumps, while the Ki-48s attacked the parked aircraft and runways.

When it was over, the Japanese destroyed at least ten P-40s on the ground and totaled nine of the transports at the two airfields, all either the C-47/C-53 or a few CNAC DC-2s. They also started fires at a fuel dump and several of the outbuildings at Chabua. Neither airfield had firefighting equipment. Once ignited the fires burned until everything had been consumed. The Japanese also cratered the paved runway at Chabua. (While cratering left the macadam runway temporarily unusable, it was quickly fixed. The craters were leveled with the gravel kicked out of them and re-rolled.)

Japanese losses were trivial: three Ki-43s were shot down, at the end of the operation when the P-40s finally got airborne. Another six were damaged. Every bomber returned.

This illustration shows Chabua at the height of the attack. The Ki-48s in the foreground have finished their bomb runs, and are getting ready to depart. A second wave of Ki-48s is coming in above the main runway, to catch what the first wave missed. Ki-43s are racing down the main taxiway strafing C-47s and C-53s in the hardstands beside the taxiway.

The first cargo-carrying flight over the Hump flew in April 1942, hauling gasoline for the Doolittle Raiders. Stored in drums lashed inside the cargo compartment of a C-47, it was the first shipment of 100 tons of 100-octane aviation gasoline brought to China in April 1942. (NMAF)

which attacked Japan nine days later, but all aircraft crashed. Regardless, the first flight over the mountains was registered, carrying the first of what would total 70 tons that April and 126 tons in May.

The aircraft Arnold promised back in March began arriving. By May 24, 19 C-47s were at Dinjan, allowing a rough-and-ready airlift to begin. These flights were disorganized. Planning was improvised. There were no navigation aids, no weather reports, no radio beacons. Pilots depended on dead reckoning using magnetic compass and indicated airspeed, while flying through monsoon-generated cloud layers. Cargoes were whatever had arrived and loaded into aircraft. Yet the tonnage carried through the end of May, meager as it was, would plummet to 25 tons, just seven flights, in June.

Several factors converged to yield the lowest-ever monthly tonnage in June 1942. In distant North Africa, Erwin Rommel's Afrika Corps captured Tobruk, opening the way to Alexandria and the Suez Canal. To prevent their capture by the Axis, reinforcements were rushed to Egypt. This included most of the Tenth Air Force, including 12 C-47s. The transports remaining in India were required in Burma.

The Japanese drive in Upper Burma cut troops there off from overland supply routes. Airlift aircraft were diverted to drop supplies to Chinese forces in northeast Burma. This included four tons of rice in May and 80 tons of supplies in June. Until Myitkyina fell it was used as a stopover to China. For the last weeks before it fell, flights there were returning to Assam, evacuating wounded and civilians. This further cut aircraft carrying supplies to China.

The low tonnage created a diplomatic crisis in July. Japan launched a major offensive in China's Zhejiang Province following the Doolittle Raid, to seize any airfields within range of Japan. Chiang also learned a plan to convert 50 B-24 bombers to C-87 transports was vetoed by Roosevelt in May. The Tenth Air Force's withdrawal and meager June tonnage left Chiang feeling betrayed. When Stilwell told Chiang the Tenth Air Force had withdrawn at a June 26 meeting, Chiang exploded.

Chiang threatened to remove China from the war. He stated that China could not continue fighting without US aid. He demanded 500 combat aircraft, 5,000 tons of supplies each month, and three US infantry divisions be sent to China if China was to continue the war.

Roosevelt knew Chiang was unlikely to withdraw from the war. He recognized Chiang wanted reassurance that China's efforts were appreciated and that Chiang was posturing to receive more assistance from the US to bolster Chiang's power. Roosevelt refused to send troops, but agreed to send warplanes and supplies, relying on airlift for the supplies. While he was willing to increase the transports sent for the airlift, through the end of 1942 any sent would be C-47s.

The aircraft initially sent, including the P-43 Lancer and P-66 Vanguard, reflected the US military's real view of China. Both fighters entered production in 1941, but were judged inadequate by the Army Air Force. Production of both aircraft ceased in 1942. Sending them to China let the US dispose of unwanted aircraft. Both looked "modern." Additionally, the

Among the aircraft sent to China was a consignment of Republic P-43 Lancer fighters. Ordered pre-war by the USAAF, their performance was inadequate for USAAF needs. They were sent to China to get rid of them. They were good enough to fight the Ki-43 on equal terms. (AC)

P-66 used the same engines as the C-47. Even if they were worthless as fighters, their engines could be used as spares on the C-47.

Spare parts shortages were a critical issue for the USAAF in 1942. Normally, when ordering aircraft, a quarter of the order's price went to spare parts. In 1939, under White House pressure to increase aircraft production, Arnold spent 100 percent of the aircraft budget on aircraft production, leaving nothing for spare parts. Tight budgets the following year left him unable to fix the shortfall that year.

By 1942 shortages were common throughout the service. The China airlift, at the end of the supply chain, felt it worse than the rest of the Army Air Force. Canny supply officers along the way siphoned off spares as they moved to Assam. Between July and September 1942, over one-third of ABC's transports were grounded due to a lack of spare parts.

The airlift slowly gained steam over the summer of 1942. A stream of pilots and aircraft found its way to Assam, even if only a trickle initially. Work on other airfields continued. Work began improving the grass field at Chabua in February 1942, with native laborers laying a crushed-stone runway – the stone crushed by hand. Work on Sookerating and Mohanbari began as soon as the monsoon abated in 1942. Work progressed despite labor shortages. The anti-British "Quit India" movement encouraged laborers to boycott British military projects.

Living conditions at the airfields was primitive, services even more so. Aircraft were fueled by hand, sometimes from five-gallon cans. No navigation beacons or radar systems were yet installed. Chabua even lacked firefighting equipment.

In early September, a new milestone was reached: the first night flight over the Hump. Its importance lay in the safety offered by darkness. Japan's night fighter capability was almost nonexistent in 1942. Since Japan began patrolling the Hump routes seeking transports once the monsoon season ended, this extra measure of safety was important.

It was balanced by the difficulty of night flight, and night's cooler temperature made icing more likely. Ice forming on the wings destroyed lift; on propellers it killed thrust. Propeller ice was also a hazard when it built up enough to be thrown off. The ice chunks bombarded the fuselage like rocks. On September 23, a C-47 bound to Chabua from Kunming crashed due to icing, killing its crew of two; the first fatalities on the Hump route.

Safety from Japanese aircraft was becoming a factor. As the monsoon season drew to a close, the IJA Air Force in Burma decided to turn its attention to the China airlift. What the Chinese and US believed important, the Japanese decided was worth stopping. Dry dirt runways permitted operations from those airfields.

The Japanese started by flying reconnaissance flights over Assam and the Fort Hertz area in late September. To stop these flights the USAAF transferred the 51st Fighter Group, equipped with P-40s, to Dinjan in October. The move yielded almost immediate results.

The C-47 and C-53 were the only USAAF transports used in the China airlift in 1942. It lacked the altitude to safely negotiate the mountain heights over the assigned northern routes. Many C-47 crews chose to take southern flight routes which could be flown at lower altitude and were shorter. (AC)

A reconnaissance Ki-46 was downed on October 19. Less than a week later, on October 25, the IJA Air Force launched a massive air attack on Dinjan and Chabua. They sent most of the available warplanes in Burma, 54 Ki-21 and Ki-48 bombers and 62 Ki-43 fighters. As a diversion they strafed Chittagong, on the Bay of Bengal, 400 miles to the southwest. To guard Burmese airfields a *sentai* based in Hanoi patrolled Lower Burma.

The Japanese arrived shortly after noon, between 1300hrs and 1400hrs local time. The Ki-21s bombed the outbuildings and support facilities, while the Ki-48s concentrated on parked aircraft and the runways. The Ki-43s split between strafing the airfields and flying cover for the attacking aircraft. Results were devastating. At Dinjan ten P-40s were destroyed on the ground. Nine transports were wrecked beyond repair. Seventeen other aircraft were damaged, but reparable.

Chabua's runway was cratered, temporarily suspending air operations there. A nearby fuel dump burned. Since Chabua then lacked firefighting equipment, fires proved hard to control. The Japanese conceded three of their aircraft shot down, with nine others damaged. It was an exchange that favored Japan.

The next day the Japanese launched a fighter sweep against Sookerating. This time they arrived just after noon. They found the 51st Group waiting for them, with P-40s airborne and spoiling for revenge. This forced the Hayabusas into fuel-consuming dogfights. Operating near the end of their effective range, they soon ran low on fuel, heading home without seriously damaging Sookerating.

A final attack was launched the next day. It did even less damage than the fighter sweep of October 26. It was the last attack on the Assam airfields in 1942. The RAF struck a major Japanese airfield near Mandalay on October 28. After that the Japanese kept more fighters closer to home against a repeat performance. That left too few Hayabusas free to provide the bombers an adequate escort.

The attacks had mixed results. Nine out of the 54 airlift C-47s were destroyed, theoretically reducing the available aircraft by one-sixth. Despite that, tonnage shipped to China in November was actually larger than the October totals. Part of this was due to improved aircrew morale. Before the raids many aircrew viewed their jobs as unimportant. They felt they were risking their lives for no good reason. Yet their mission had let the Japanese try to stop them. Aircrew concluded there was more to their job than they believed. They were more willing to push on to complete a mission and less willing to abort a flight.

In October 1942 the IJA Air Force launched a series of bombing raids against the Assam airfields forming the Indian terminus of the Hump. Both Ki-21 (shown here) and Ki-48 bombers participated in these attacks. Although initially successful, subsequent raids caused little damage and saw high Japanese casualties. (AC)

The US set up an early warning system to alert the airfields of incoming attacks. This had been badly needed, but neglected prior to the Japanese attacks. Now the problem was dealt with. Since the hills inhibited radar effectiveness, a series of radio-equipped observation posts was set up 50 to 75 miles from the Assam airfields. This provided 20 to 30 minutes advanced warning of incoming attacks, enough to scramble fighters.

The Japanese attacks proved better than "Quit India" in discouraging local employment at US airfields. Many native workers quit after the attacks, deciding they were not paid enough to be bombed and shot at. They were eventually replaced, but a near-term labor shortage resulted.

Despite progress made since April, only a trickle of supplies made it to China by air. While the US pledged to send 5,000 tons of supplies each month, from the time the airlift started until the end of November the aggregate tonnage of what actually arrived in China was only 40 percent of that. Most of what was sent in 1942 was aviation fuel and ammunition to support what became the US Fourteenth Air Force, operating out of China. A complete overhaul and reorganization of the airlift was needed. It occurred on December 1, 1942, when the Air Transport Command took charge.

Air Transport Command takes over: December 1942 to September 1943

Arnold, in Washington, had been dissatisfied with the performance of the Assam-Burma Ferry Command for several months. They were failing to deliver the goods. It was not all their fault. Despite orders, the Tenth Air Force was constantly diverting airlift aircraft to other tasks. Some was, though. The combat pilots running the ABC knew how to plan and run bombing missions, but were inexperienced at running what was essentially a cargo airline.

Arnold sought ways to reform the ABC. In July he recommended CNAC take over management of the airlift, running their own and the USAAF aircraft flying the airlift. Stilwell, ever suspicious of the Chinese, vetoed the idea. Arnold sought another solution. He got it when C. R. Smith submitted a report on improving the airlift.

Prewar, Smith, at age 35, was president of American Airlines, one of the US's major civilian airlines. In March 1942 Arnold replaced the ailing head of Ferry Command, running all the AAF's transports, with Colonel Harold George. George knew nothing about air transport. Unlike most combat aviators, he knew that, and asked for an operations director who did. Arnold recruited Smith, commissioning Smith an AAF colonel. Roosevelt nationalized

Brigadier General C.R. Smith (left) was recruited into the Army Air Force from American Airlines in 1942. Chief of staff at Air Transport Command, he was an architect of Hump operations. He is shown at the Casablanca Conference with President Roosevelt's sons, LtC Elliott Roosevelt (center) and Lt Franklin Roosevelt, Jr. (right). (USNHHC)

all civilian airliners into military service on December 15, 1941, so the job was a good fit for Smith.

Equally, Smith was a good fit for the job. Like George he knew what he did not know – he knew nothing about the Army or military aviation. But Smith knew airline operations better than anyone else, and George filled in Smith's gaps in military knowledge. It was a perfect paring.

Smith filled Ferry Command with airline executives. He also replaced the crisis management attitude common to combat officers with a culture of mission efficiency. In fall 1942, he turned his attention to the China airlift, the problem child in USAAF military transportation. By then the Air Ferry Command had become the Air Transport Command, better reflecting their real role. Its primary responsibility had altered from ferrying aircraft to air transportation.

Smith's October report on the China airlift stated 7,500 tons per month could be carried by 75 transports, if the airlift was operated efficiently, along the lines of an airline. This contrasted with the belief of Brigadier General Clayton Bissell, commanding the Tenth Air Force after Brereton's departure for Africa in June. Bissell felt 5,000 tons represented an upper limit for air cargo.

Smith recommended ATC take over the airlift, with ATC creating a new organization dedicated to the India to China flights. Arnold preferred Smith's approach to Bissell's. Arnold gave ATC the job. On December 1, 1942, the 1st Ferry Group was transferred from the Tenth Air Force to the ATC and renamed the India-China Wing. Brigadier General Edward Alexander assumed command. The ICW reported to ATC headquarters in Washington, cutting the Tenth Air Force out of the command structure. The Tenth Air Force kept responsibility for defending airlift airfields and protecting transports along the route. It lacked operational authority over ICW aircraft.

When Alexander took over, the ICW had 60 C-47s. They were soon joined by a dozen C-87s, the first of which arrived in January. Only two ICW airfields, Chabua and Dinjan, had gravel-paved runways, and only Chabua had the hardened runway C-87s needed to operate from. All needed paved hardstands where aircraft could park for servicing and loading/unloading. Without these the aircrafts' tires would sink into the mud of the dirt hardstands when the monsoon rains began in May. Alexander headquartered the ICW at Chabua.

Alexander intended to divide the transports evenly between the four airfields available to him to reduce the chance Japan could take out most of his aircraft in one raid. Instead he was forced to concentrate the C-87s at Chabua, sending most C-47s to Dinjan and the more primitive Mohanbari and Sookerating. The Japanese were the smallest threat to the C-87s however. All of the first six Expresses arriving at Chabua were lost in flying accidents by August – three without trace between April 9 and May 7.

The reorganization had immediate positive effects. Tonnage arriving in China in December 1942 almost doubled what was sent in November, increased slightly in January, and more than doubled January's total in February. Two contributing factors were that Alexander made night flights routine, increasing the total possible flights and he set flight schedules. Pilots were told when to fly and not permitted to abort due to weather.

The first C-87s began arriving in Assam in January 1943. They started crashing shortly after arrival. By August 1943 all six of the first-arriving C-87s had crashed, three without a trace. Although hard to fly, many more were sent to fly the airlift. They had a large cargo capacity and were available. (LOC)

Another factor was improved communications and the addition of navigation aids. By the end of February, Kunming established direct radio communications with Australia. Previously communications with Washington traveled across India, from there across Africa to South America to be relayed to Washington from Brazil. The network, especially across Africa, was archaic. Communications frequently went astray or never arrived. The radio chain from Brisbane, Australia east to Washington was shorter and more mature.

A low-power homing beacon became operational at Fort Hertz in January. It was short range, only 20 miles, and only provided a compass heading. Fort Hertz marked the midpoint of the route, and was as far south as it was then safe to fly. Aircraft hearing it knew roughly where they were and not to stray further south. In April six direction-finding stations were installed in India and China, at the principal airlift airfields. These were short range, but helped plots find the airfields.

More transports helped. Arnold visited China in early February. The trip gave him a greater appreciation for the difficulties faced by pilots (his aircraft got lost, arriving at Kunming four hours late), and the challenges the airlift offered. Afterwards he doubled the number of transports assigned to the ICW, raising it to 125. He also decided to minimize US personnel in China. Additional warplanes sent to China should be flown by Chinese pilots, trained by USAAF instructors as necessary.

Arnold assigned Alexander an interim target of 4,000 tons of cargo monthly. This was significantly lower than the 5,000 tons Chiang demanded or the 10,000 monthly tons (rising to 50,000 tons by December) ATC planners assumed could be carried. Deliveries were split between Chiang, Stilwell (now US ground force commander in China), and Claire Chennault, the former AVG commander heading the Tenth Air Force detachment in China. Stilwell demanded 3,683 tons each month to outfit "Yoke Force" (a US-trained Chinese ground formation), while Chennault needed the airlift to bring his aircraft in China munitions and fuel. Arnold's target was realistic; achievable once Alexander got his promised aircraft.

Alexander would not reach the 4,000-ton target until August, much less 50,000 tons by December. Bissell was part of the problem. While he could no longer "borrow" airlift aircraft, he controlled traffic to the airlift airfields. Instead of sending Alexander cargoes Alexander wanted, Bissell arbitrarily changed priorities on what was sent to the Assam airfields.

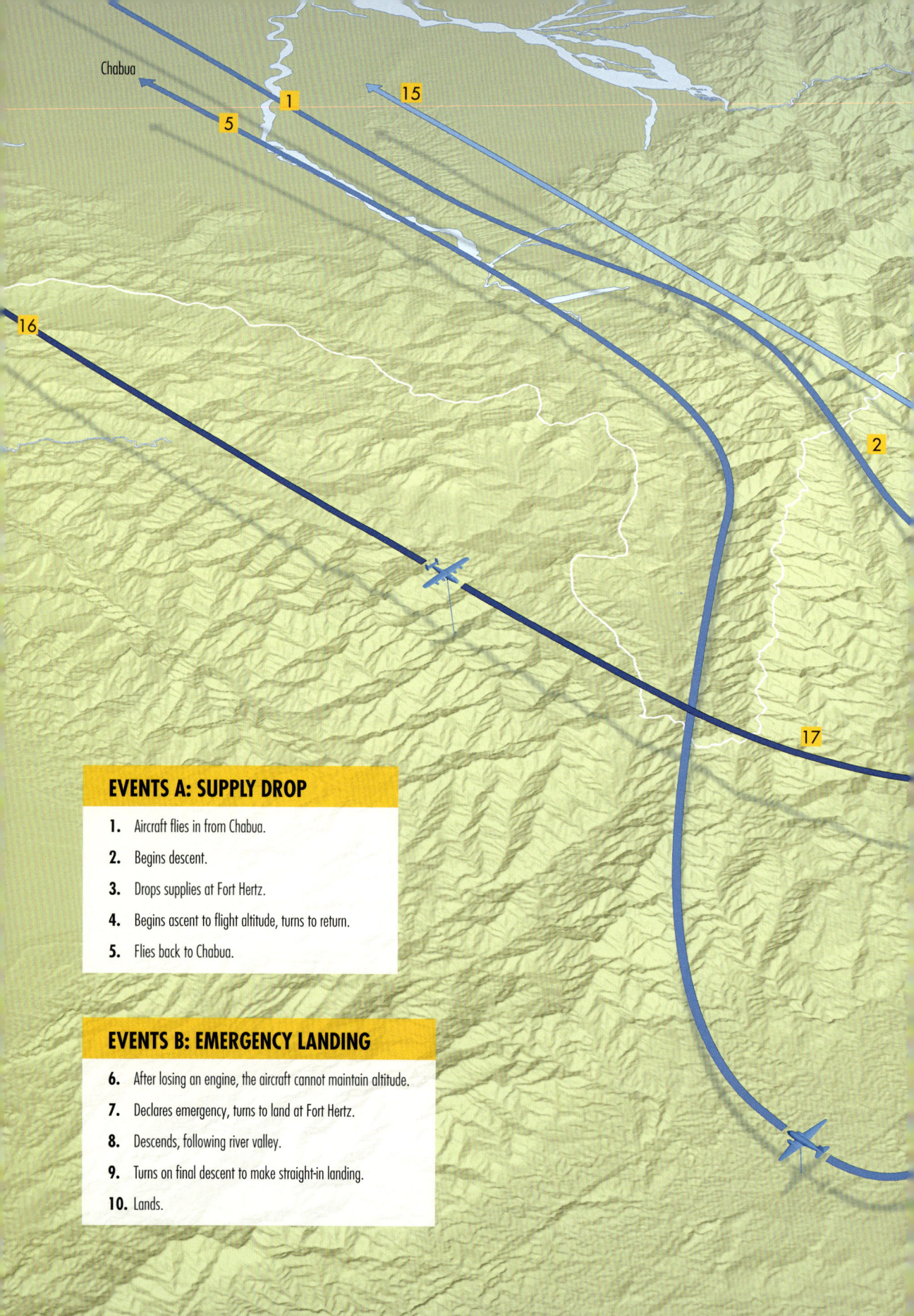

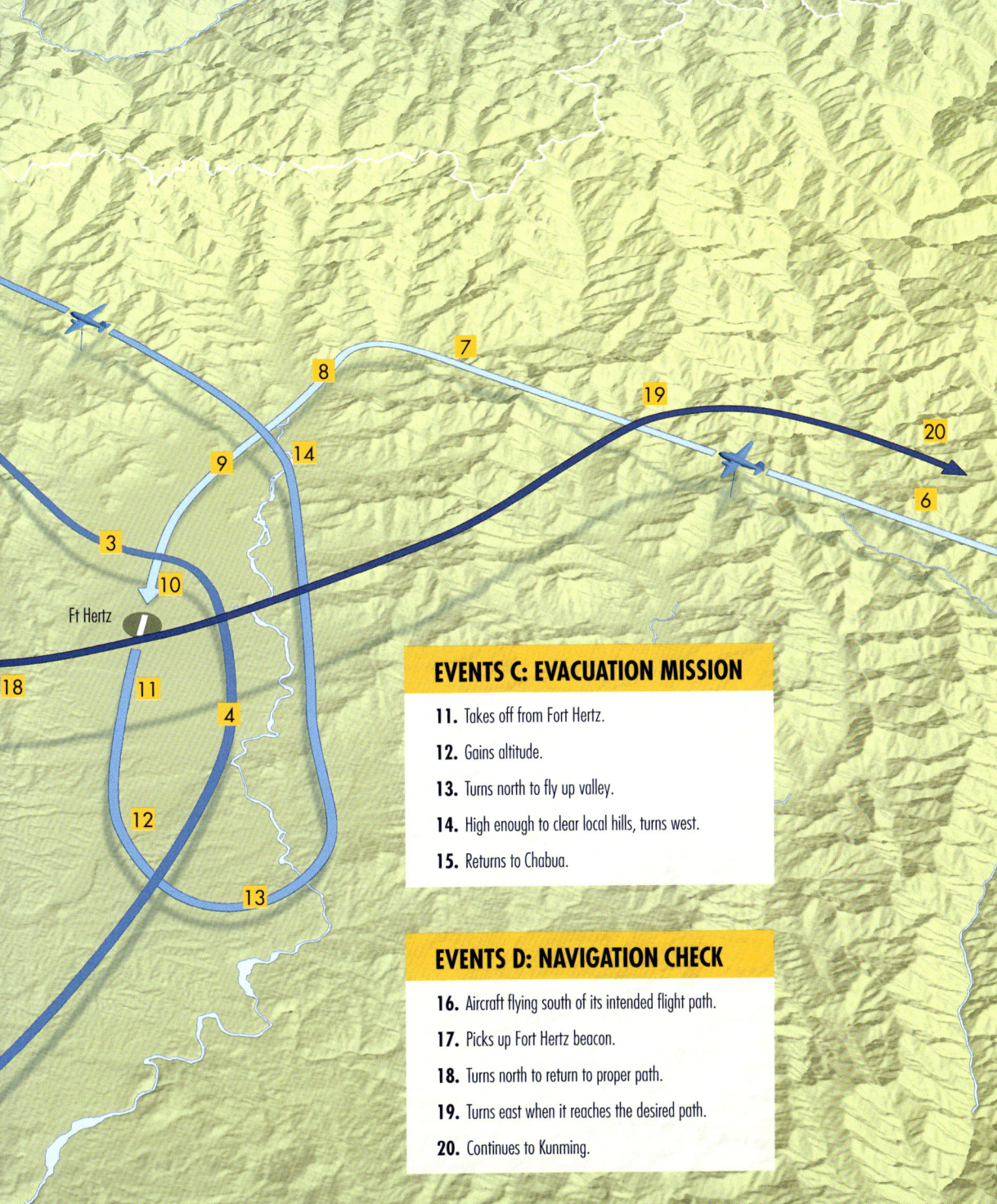

The Fort Hertz bolt-hole

Fort Hertz was a British-held Northern Burma outpost. In August 1942 a British reconnaissance mission discovered it was still in British hands. An airfield was cleared and the base turned into a hidden outpost en route to China. It served as an emergency airstrip and had a navigation beacon.

EVENTS C: EVACUATION MISSION

11. Takes off from Fort Hertz.
12. Gains altitude.
13. Turns north to fly up valley.
14. High enough to clear local hills, turns west.
15. Returns to Chabua.

EVENTS D: NAVIGATION CHECK

16. Aircraft flying south of its intended flight path.
17. Picks up Fort Hertz beacon.
18. Turns north to return to proper path.
19. Turns east when it reaches the desired path.
20. Continues to Kunming.

Worse, he siphoned off some of the cargoes arriving in India. Engines and spare parts sent to the ICW ended up redirected to Tenth Air Force warplanes, despite protests by George in Washington. The problem was finally resolved when Bissell was transferred in August 1943.

Two strategic meetings held in early 1943 shaped the airlift; the Casablanca Conference held in January and the May Trident Conference in Washington, D. C. At Casablanca, Roosevelt, Churchill (Great Britain's Prime Minister), and the heads of the US and British military met to set the strategic direction of the war. The conference tabled proposals by Stilwell and Chennault to expand the ground and air efforts in China, but decided to expand supply deliveries to both China and the Soviet Union.

At the conference Arnold stated it was possible to deliver 10,000 tons a month via an airlift. This fit Roosevelt's hopes of attacking Japan by air through China. It also led to the creation of the Fourteenth Air Force in China that spring, under Chennault. The Tenth Air Force was split, retaining units in India while Chennault's Fourteenth Air Force took the ones based in China.

At Trident, Stilwell and Chennault offered competing visions of how to use China. Chennault recommended outfitting 102 Chinese ground divisions through airlifted supplies. Chennault stated that with 400 to 450 aircraft and 4,000 to 7,000 tons of supplies each month, the Fourteenth Air Force could conduct an air offensive which would end with heavy bombers attacking Japan. Both men were wildly optimistic. Chiang lacked 102 reliable divisions to outfit, while Chennault's offensive required airfields that could be easily taken by the Japanese if China-based aircraft threatened Japan.

As with Casablanca, Trident was attended by Roosevelt, Churchill, and the chiefs of both US and British armed forces. Roosevelt hammered out a compromise between the Stilwell and Chennault plans. It largely favored Chennault. Roosevelt agreed to send the requested aircraft and provide 7,000 tons of supplies per month to China by July. Chennault would get the first 4,700 tons, while Stilwell got the balance.

Stilwell's 102-division fantasy was shelved, but he was permitted to continue equipping and training Yoke Force, three Chinese divisions in Yunnan Province. They would be the spearhead of an offensive to retake Upper Burma in late 1943 and reopen the Burma Road. Stilwell remained unconvinced an airlift could move as much supplies as a highway.

A line of Chinese troops marches down a road in the Salween Valley. These are part of the Chinese force brought to India for training at General Joseph Stilwell's instigation. At one time, Stilwell proposed equipping and training 102 Chinese divisions even though China lacked 102 reliable divisions. (LOC)

The first C-46 Commandos arrived in March 1943. The aircraft offered promise. It carried twice the load of a C-47. While it eventually became the backbone of the airlift, until the problems were wrung out of it, it was unreliable and crash-prone. It took a year to deliver on its promise. (NMAF)

Trident provided Alexander with strategic purpose for the rest of 1943. "Ten thousand tons by December" became the new goal. Prospects of actually flying 7,000 tons of supplies in July were low. It required everything to go right and nothing wrong, plus a lot more aircraft.

Aircraft were on their way. The Army Air Force had a new transport, the C-46. While it would become the iconic Hump aircraft, in spring 1943 it was brand new. The C-46 was a cargo-hauler, while the smaller C-47 was badly needed to carry troops, especially paratroopers. With a world-wide shortage of C-47s, Arnold decided to phase out and replace the additional C-47s to be sent to the airlift with the larger C-46s. They were sent as they were delivered to the Air Force, ten in March, 20 more in April, and ten more each of the following months until 50 were flying the Hump.

On paper this looked good. The C-46 carried twice the load of the C-47 using the same crew. It had a greater range and higher ceiling. Yet it had been rushed into production, going straight from the drawing board to the assembly line without a prototype. Most passed pre-delivery inspection by ignoring downcheck issues. The C-46 was immature, with multiple problems that took a year to resolve. While the new transport did not worry the Japanese, initially it thoroughly frightened its crew and passengers.

Other factors conspired to keep the tonnage lower than desired through the first three quarters of 1943. There were pilot shortages. Aircrew were not supposed to fly more than 100 hours in a month. That meant to keep aircraft flying at peak rates required two sets of aircrew for each transport. Through much of spring the ratio was 1.6:1, not the desired 2:1. Otherwise flyable aircraft sat on the ground because no one was available to fly them.

The aircrew shortage was aggravated by "Humpitis," anxiety neurosis with regard to flying the Hump. Fatigue from spending too many hours in the air, combined with the nervous tension caused by the hazards of the flight (which included extreme weather, getting lost due to poor navigation aids, and the risk of encountering enemy aircraft), combined to create flying fatigue and ultimately fear of flying.

Flying hours were limited to reduce this kind of fatigue, but after months flying the Hump it developed anyway. Rotating pilots out of the Hump routes to less-stressful trans-India routes or sending men to rest camps helped aircrew recover. Aircrew shortages sometimes prevented these reliefs, which in turn aggravated aircrew shortages by leading to increases in pilots collapsing.

The monsoon season's start also reduced tonnage. The rain turned dirt or grass runways into quagmires into which aircraft tires sank axle deep. Full loads could be flown only

The US sent a lot of construction equipment to the CBI. This included air-portable bulldozers like the one shown here. They could be carried by glider or transport to a rough grass field and then quickly carve out a runway large enough for C-47s and C-46s to operate on. (NMAF)

from paved runways. There were only two paved runways through September 1943, one at Dinjan and one at Chabua. There were also only 14 paved hardstands. Dirt runways at Mohanbari and Sookerating could be used by C-47s, but only if they reduced takeoff weight and freight carried to China.

Airfield construction was controlled by the RAF. Through June 1943, the Assam airfields had a low priority. Work progressed slowly. General Archibald Wavell, commanding British forces in India, refused to increase airfield construction priority unless ordered to by London. London, busy running the rest of the war, neglected sending them. The US sent aviation construction units from the US to Assam in June, but they would not start work until late August.

The result was tonnage was anemic through the end of the monsoon season, bouncing around between 1,900 and 2,400 tons through June. Tonnage increased during the summer months and into September as a result of the aftermath of the Trident Conference, but it never reached 7,000 tons per month. September, with 5,125 tons carried, was the best that could be done. Dry weather following the end of the monsoon season promised better conditions, but good weather was not the only thing arriving in October. So did the Japanese.

The Japanese offensives: October 1943 to May 1944

October began with a new leader for the ICW. Alexander was relieved, officially for health reasons, as September ended. In reality, he was replaced because the ICW never met its tonnage targets during his tenure. The ATC doubled the ICW's aircrew manpower, starting in June, building to a total of 535 aircrew (pilot, co-pilot, and radio operator – C-87s also needed a flight engineer). Yet Alexander never reached half the tonnage expected. Washington decided inadequate leadership was the triggering cause for failure. New leadership was needed. Brigadier General Earl Hoag relieved Alexander on October 15. Hoag brought Colonel Thomas Hardin with him to command the ICW's eastern sector, responsible for the Assam-China leg. Hardin arrived a month before Hoag.

Hardin was a rare bird in the USAAF, an airline executive with military experience. He joined the Signal Corps in 1918, and served in France during World War I. He remained in the reserves postwar, earning wings in 1922. He then moved into commercial aviation. He served on the predecessor to the National Transportation Safety Board (the Independent Air Safety Board) in the late 1930s, joining TWA as a vice president in 1940, returning to the AAF after the US entered World War II. He was a colleague and friend of C. R. Smith. Hardin had a reputation as someone who could successfully tackle difficult jobs. Smith sent him to India to get the airlift humming.

Hardin hit Assam like a whirlwind. He obtained a worn-out B-25 as his personal aircraft, using it to skip between the six Assam airfields under his charge and from Assam to China. (In addition to the four airlift airfields, Eastern Sector Missamari and Jorhat belonged to his command.) He flew in all weather, often the only pilot.

His aircrews feared him. Hardin set load and load placement standards immediately upon arrival. He expected his subordinates to meet the operational standards and goals he set. If they failed, either by not doing something Hardin directed or by doing something wrong, he relieved and replaced them. Pilots failing to meet flying schedules were disciplined.

According to legend, Hardin declared "there was no weather on the Hump unless he said so." He never made such a statement, but it fit the mood he tried to set. His men respected him despite his abrasive edge. He never asked them to do anything he was unwilling to do himself. His efforts led to an immediate tonnage jump, from 5,125 in September to 7,240 in October.

On October 25, the new regime created a new Search and Rescue Squadron. Based in Chabua, and overseen by Wing Intelligence and Security, it reviewed reports of crashed planes. It also used the two B-25s and two C-47s it owned to survey crash

Hayabusa trap

When the Japanese launched Operation *Tsuzigiri*, the USAAF looked for ways to counter the Japanese fighter sweeps. The Fourteenth Air Force had several squadrons of B-24 bombers stationed in China. The B-24 closely resembled the C-87 transports flying the Hump. The C-87 was a cargo variant of the B-24. The C-87's fuselage was a little longer, and it lacked the turrets, but from a distance they looked identical, especially with the early versions of the B-24, which had a glass nose, the same shape as the nose cone of the C-87.

The one big difference between the two was the B-24 was heavily armed. The B-24D carried 11 .50cal machine guns, six in three twin power turrets and five in flexible single mounts in the waist and nose. This was at least five times the armament of the Ki-43, which carried two 12.7mm machine guns at most. (Some Ki-43s in Burma had two 7.9mm machine guns or one 7.7mm and one 12.7mm machine gun.) This led Claire Chennault, commander of the Fourteenth Air Force, to set a trap for the Hayabusas.

He had the 308th Bombardment Squadron – which flew B-24s in loose groups of two to six – fly the routes being attacked by the *Tsuzigiri* fighters in the hope they would mistake the bombers for the unarmed C-87. He felt the sight of a formation of what appeared to be C-87s would prove irresistible to the Japanese. Colonel William Fisher, commanding the 308th, and his B-24 crews eagerly fell in with the plan.

They began flying between China and India, along routes followed by C-87s. Flying to India, they just carried extra ammunition and enough fuel to reach Assam. On the way back they carried extra fuel to make up for what they had burned flying to India. They also took advantage of the opportunity to bring critically needed items for their squadron on a space-available basis.

The hook was well-baited and set. On October 27, the Japanese bit down on it, hard. A sweep of eight Ki-43s spotted one group of bombers flying a decoy mission. As expected, the 50th Sentai Hayabusas, led by Captain Hashimoto, mistook them for C-87s. Seven Ki-43s moved in for the kill. The eighth could not eject its drop tanks and broke off.

The result is shown in this illustration. The attacking Hayabusas flew into a buzz saw of .50cal fire. Several Ki-43s were hit by the B-24s' guns. Two crash-landed in the Burmese jungle. One of the pilots was captured by locals and turned over to the Allies as a prisoner. The other managed to walk to a Japanese-held outpost.

The B-24 flight claimed to have shot down all eight Hayabusas that attacked it. The exaggeration is understandable. Once the Japanese realized their opponents were shooting back they broke off the attack. Watching the Ki-43s diving away at high speed led gunners to believe they were crashing.

The Japanese ended Operation *Tsuzigiri* after two more days, claiming they were burning too much gasoline to continue it. During that time the 308th claimed another ten Ki-43s shot down and probably got two or three more.

General Thomas Hardin assumed command of eastern operations of the India-China Wing in October 1943. He transformed the faltering airlift into a successful effort during his year in command there, achieving the 10,000 ton monthly goal within two months of his arrival. This shows him at his office in Chabua. (Wikipedia)

sites. These aircraft could airdrop supplies to survivors. It also had two two-passenger L-5 liaison aircraft capable of landing on improvised runways to evacuate survivors, especially wounded survivors. It increased survival rates among crash survivors and improved aircrew morale.

October brought the return of the Japanese. The airlift was becoming big enough for them to notice. Japan had shut the last route to China, but the US had reopened it. By fall, the airlift carried more tonnage per month than the Burma Road did before the Japanese closed it. While the Japanese may not have known the exact tonnage totals, they knew it was significant enough to improve Chinese morale. Moreover US aircraft in China were beginning to attack Japanese resources there.

Monsoon weather prevented a serious air operation from Burma over the summer. Instead, Japan opened their anti-air campaign in June 1943, hiring a Chinese agent inside Kuomintang-controlled China to conduct a sabotage campaign against the US. The agent started his campaign in August. He was quickly caught in Chungking before August ended and was executed.

They also set up false homing beacons in Upper Burma, hoping to lure transports off-course, and exhaust their fuel before reaching their destination. That did not work either. The Japanese could not get their beacons to work reliably. The US pilots also routinely ignored their own beacons in 1943, except at their destinations. Most Hump pilots then lacked the training and proficiency with beacon navigation to use it successfully except for flying directly to an airfield. They flew without using it, relying on dead reckoning instead.

Once the weather cleared, in late October the IJA Air Force launched an interdiction campaign on the India-China air highway. Called Operation *Tsuzigiri* (Street Murder in Japanese), it had flights of eight Ki-43s patrolling the skies around Fort Hertz in far Northern Burma. They staged out of Myitkyina. Their hunting ground was over Sumprabum, 50 miles south of Fort Hertz. After each patrol, they refueled at Myitkyina and returned to home bases in Lower Burma, safe from reprisal.

All Hump flights were supposed to fly north of Fort Hertz, but that required a longer route over higher mountains. The direct, shorter route went over Sumprabum, and ICW pilots used this short cut with increasing frequency over the summer months. It was quicker, and absent of a Japanese fighter presence, safer than the prescribed route. Planes were less likely to hit a mountain, and the Japanese were not around. Transports were slower than the Ki-43. Their unarmed survival depended on not being found. Even the Ki-43's indifferent armament could shoot down a laden transport.

When the Japanese flew their first *Tsuzigiri* sweep on October 13 they found and attacked three transports, a C-47, a C-46, and a C-87. The C-47 and C-87 were shot down. The Japanese tried again. On October 20, they downed one C-46 and two C-46s on October 23. A C-46 was shot down on October 27.

The US reacted by laying a trap for the Japanese. The China-based 308th Bombardment Squadron flew B-24s, similar in appearance to the C-87. Hoping the Japanese would mistake the heavily armed bombers for the unarmed transports, Chennault asked Colonel William Fisher, commanding the 308th, to lure the Japanese into attacking the bombers. Fisher had his aircraft fly together in loose formation between Assam and China carrying extra .50cal ammunition. They also carried extra fuel on the China-bound legs to make up what they used on the decoy flights.

The trap was sprung on October 27. Shortly after shooting down a C-46, the Japanese spotted a formation of what they thought were C-87s. They swooped in to discover their quarry was not unarmed transports. One fighter could not eject its drop tank, and broke off. Two others were so badly damaged they could not reach Myitkyina and made forced landings, destroying their planes.

The 308th continued flying the route over the next three days. They claimed eight Japanese fighters downed on October 27 and ten more over the next three days. In reality the Japanese 50th Sentai lost only three aircraft. Additionally Tenth Air Force P-40 fighter-bombers bombed Myitkyina on October 31 to prevent its use as a staging base.

The Japanese discontinued the *Tsuzigiri* sweeps when October ended. Even three planes downed represented heavy losses. More important was the logistical toll of the operation. The *Tsuzigiri* flights burned a lot of gasoline for meager results. Fuel was burned patrolling the skies north of Myitkyina. Even more was burned flying to and from Myitkyina and the Burmese coast, where the airfields were located. In exchange the 50th Sentai bagged only six transports. The Japanese could not afford the fuel.

Tsuzigiri's biggest impact was altering transport pilot behavior. They went back to flying the recommended route well north of Fort Hertz. Temporarily. After several weeks without a Japanese aerial presence over Upper Burma, pilots once again started flying the southerly straight-line path between China and Burma.

Next the Japanese returned to bombing the Chinese and Assam airfields from which the airlift flights originated. They launched over 30 raids against both sets of airfields throughout 1943, perhaps half of which were against the Assam airfields. Yet these raids were riskier than the ones in 1942, one reason they tried *Tsuzigiri*. The US improved their defenses during the winter. In February 1942 an attack by 40 Japanese aircraft was intercepted by 32 P-40s. The Japanese lost over one-quarter of the attacking force.

Hardin established a dedicated Search and Rescue Squadron shortly after arriving. Its mission was to find and assist survivors from crashes. It worked with locals, such as the scout on the right, to lead downed fliers like the man on the left to safety. The survivor, in stockings and injured, is happy. (NMAF)

Operation *Tsuzigiri* saw the IJA Air Force send fighter sweeps to hunt transports flying to and from China. Initially successful, it was called off after the Fourteenth Air Force began laying ambushes for the Ki-43s flying the sweeps. Hump pilots shifted north to avoid the Japanese, eliminating potential victims. (Wikipedia)

OPPOSITE OPERATION *U-GO*, MARCH–JUNE 1944

With *Tsuzigiri*'s failure, the Japanese had no effective way to strike at the airlift. Although they made some 15 attacks in October and November, these did little damage. This included one major raid against Dinjan on December 13. The Fifth Air Army sent 20 bombers and 25 fighters, hitting it before defending P-40s intercepted them. They still did little damage and were caught by US fighters after the attack, losing six bombers and three fighters. (The US claimed 12 and five downed.) As 1944 started, Allied air power in India and Burma had grown enough that the IJA Air Force was pushed on the defensive.

A third summit meeting was held in November 1943 in Cairo, Egypt, notable mainly because in addition to Roosevelt and Churchill, Chiang also attended, the only one in which he was present. There Chiang repeated demands for 10,000 tons of cargo shipped monthly to China by air. He also agreed to support an invasion of Northern Burma by an American-trained Chinese division, to support a British invasion of Lower Burma in early 1944. After the invasion date was pushed to November 1944, Chiang reversed his decision.

Night flying increased in November, made possible when torches used as landing lights were replaced with generator-powered electrical lights. Increased night flying increased tonnage, but also increased accident rates. Average loss rate of aircraft by accidents jumped from five per month from June to October to 19 in November. Experience, and possibly natural selection, reduced the total back down to five per month in subsequent months.

Also started in 1943 was a fuel pipeline from Calcutta, which connected to the Assam airfields and Ledo by the end of 1943. Pipeline was airlifted to Kunming and Fort Hertz starting in September. The pipeline connected Calcutta to Kunming by January 1945, paralleling the Ledo and Burma Roads. The Ledo Road, started at Ledo, India in March 1943, eventually ran to Loiwing, Burma, where it connected with the old Burma Road.

Hardin was given 16 C-47s and 40 C-46s to carry pipeline. When pipeline was unavailable, these aircraft carried other airlift cargoes, increasing cargo capacity. Hardin was also allowed to borrow 24 B-24s to carry cargo in December. The result was a total tonnage of 12,590 carried in December, the first time the 10,000-ton goal was surpassed. It was a breakthrough. Thereafter, except for March 1944, monthly tonnage always exceeded 10,000 tons.

US success increased Japanese desire to cut off the airlift. As Allied air power increased in Burma and the provinces surrounding it, Japanese air power was slowly dwindling. The Japanese lacked the aircraft to stop the airlift. Instead, they decided to launch a ground offensive into India to cut the Allied supply line to the Assam airfields.

Japan had not attempted this in 1942 or 1943 because they did not believe it possible to supply an army entering India from the Burmese border. There were no railroads, the rivers were unfavorable and the roads crossing the border were more accurately described as trails. They revised that judgment due to the Chindits.

A light infantry formation raised in India, the Chindits specialized in jungle warfare, penetrating the Burmese jungles on foot. Resupply and heavy weapons were conducted by airdrop or hacking out airstrips in the

The Chindits convinced the Imperial Army that invading India was possible, even without conventional supply lines. To the Japanese, the Chindits moved effortlessly through the jungles. Unaware of Chindit losses, the Japanese commander in Burma decided to employ similar infiltration tactics to cut the supply lines of the Assam airfields. (Wikipedia)

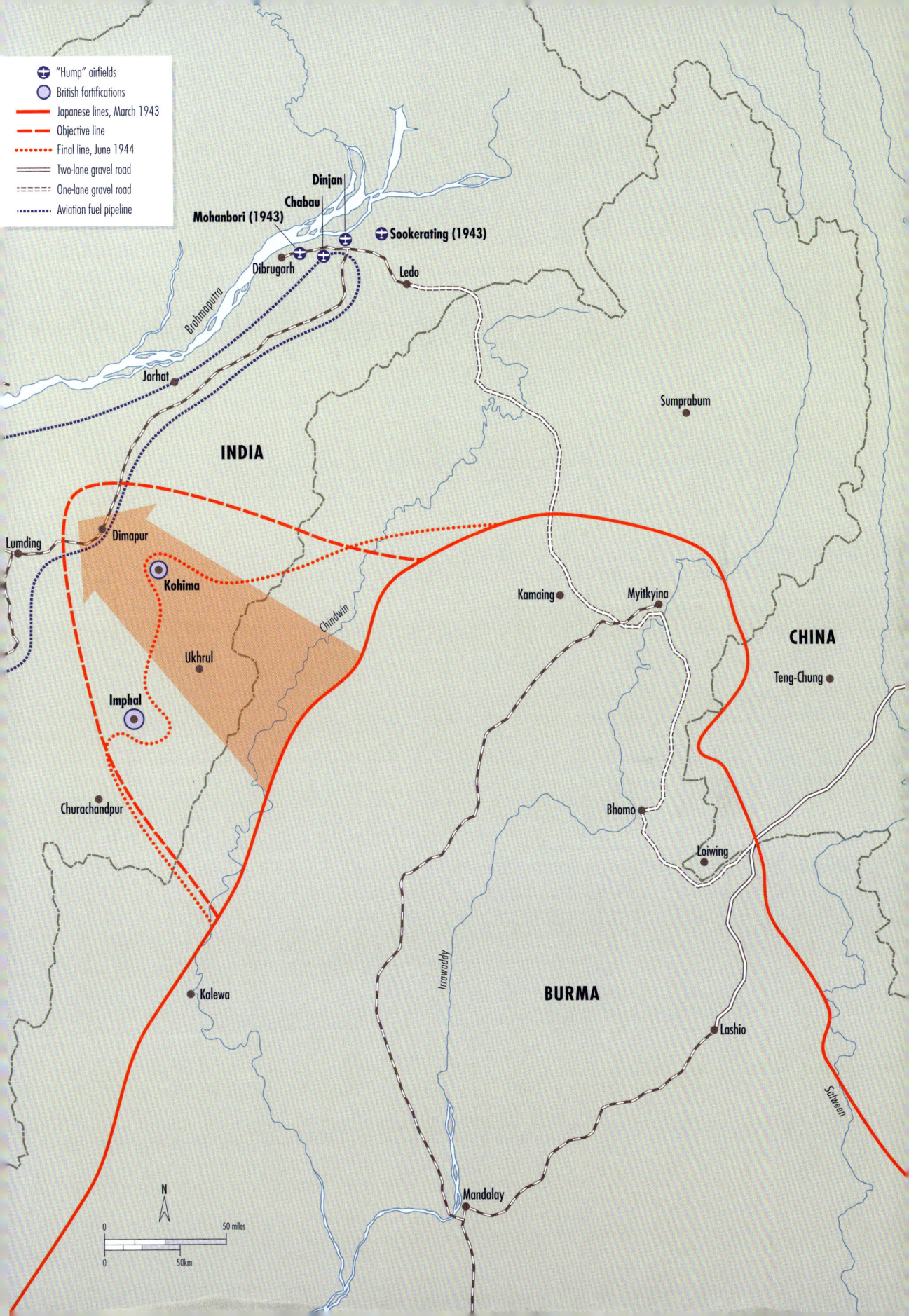

Airlift offered enormous advantages to the Allies in the jungles and mountains of the CBI. Airdrops kept troops supplied in the absence of conventional supply lines. By 1944 besieged garrisons and infiltration units could rely on necessary supplies arriving by air, freeing them from dependence on ground-based supply lines. (AC)

jungle for transports to land. With no supply lines, they could move through previously impenetrable jungle. Ironically, the concept was inspired by the way Japanese troops moved through Malaya to capture Singapore. The Allies assumed the Japanese were jungle-fighting experts.

In reality the Japanese Home Islands were temperate, climate closer to Washington State than Malaya. Jungles were alien. Their movement through Southeast Asia was improvised. But having seen the Chindits penetrate the Burmese frontier, the Japanese concluded they could move into Assam the same way. They decided to launch an invasion south of Assam and move deep enough into India to capture Dimapur, a major British supply center. The Japanese believed this would cut the supply route to the airfields.

The offensive, which the Japanese called *U-Go*, was launched in early March 1944. Four infantry divisions (including one Indian National Army unit) and a tank regiment launched drives aimed at Imphal and Kohima. The route took the Japanese across the Naga Hills, mountainous terrain with few roads or routes capable of being used as supply lines. Initially successful, the Japanese forced the British back on Imphal and surrounded and besieged Kohima. The British and Indian units dug in and held. While isolated overland, they were resupplied by airdrop, allowing them to hang on until relief reached them.

Aerial resupply did not shrink China tonnage. The ICW had sufficient transports maintain Hump tonnage while supporting resupply missions. By the start of 1944, the Tenth Air Force had sufficient resources to support land operations in multiple ways: close air support, aerial resupply, airlift of troops behind enemy lines, and evacuation of wounded. They embraced these roles enthusiastically.

By contrast, the Japanese troops found themselves isolated by the Naga Hills. They too could not be supplied overland. Lacking air superiority or transport aircraft, they could not be resupplied by air. The Japanese soldiers starved and ran low on ammunition. The offensive culminated in April, with the failure to take Imphal or Kohima. Defeated in May, by June surviving Japanese were heading back to Burma. With its failure, the last opportunity for Japan to stop the airlift passed. Thereafter the Japanese were increasingly on the defensive. The air road to China became increasingly easier.

Maturing the airlift: June 1944 to November 1944

Japan's India offensive testified to the success of the airlift in 1944. Throughout 1944's first five months, the airlift had gathered momentum. More transports were part of the reason; there were well over 300 transports by spring 1944 in the ICA, but operations were constrained by shortages. There were too few pilots. By April there were occasional fuel shortages at the airlift airfields. Planes sat idle as a result. When there were pilots and fuel, labor shortages at the airfields delayed flights due to an inability to load the aircraft. While monthly tonnage remained above 10,000 tons through May, growth flatlined.

The India-China Wing had grown. In July it was reorganized into the India-China Division (ICD). The sections under it were raised to wings, with a fourth wing added to existing India, Assam, and China wings. A new Bengal Wing was added. Each controlled traffic within their areas.

Infrastructure improvements implemented in the first months of 1944 eased roadblocks. More airfield runways and hardstands were paved by the time the 1944 monsoon started. In April Hardin, who replaced Hoag as head of the ICD after Hoag went to Europe, asked the US Army for 2,500 logistics troops to load and unload aircraft, with 1,000 to be sent immediately. An air traffic control system was set up.

When 1944 started, there was no route structure. Pilots plotted their routes independently. Arrivals occurred haphazardly, with multiple aircraft appearing at an airport nearly together. This led to landing delays. Aircraft waited in holding patterns waiting for previous arrivals to land first. Sometimes circling for hours, aircraft burned fuel that with better planning would have been available for use in China. Without a reliable route structure, pilots got lost and crashed, either by flying into a mountain or running out of fuel.

A combination of labor shortages and absence of mechanization in India led to methods of loading aircraft considered unconventional elsewhere. This included using elephants as living cargo cranes. Here an elephant carries a standard 55-gallon fuel drum weighing 425lbs into the cargo bay of a C-46. (AC)

To improve navigation, Radio Range stations replaced the low-power navigation beacons at the primary airfields. With significantly longer range, they covered most of the flight path between India and China. Gaps were eventually filled by installing Radio Range stations in Burma. Radio Range worked well over Assam's flat Brahmaputra Valley, where the Assam airfields were. The hills of Upper Burma and Yunnan Province could deflect signals, making its use difficult there.

The stations allowed approach procedures to be developed controlling arriving and departing aircraft. Formal air traffic control (ATC) rules were established. Airfields had control towers where ATC controllers could observe and direct traffic into and out of the field. Pilots followed designated approach paths to an airfield, contacting the tower when coming in to land. The tower then instructed the pilot when and how to land. Airfield control was a critical element in avoiding midair and taxiway collisions as flight rates increased. By November 1944, aircraft were landing and lifting off from Kunming every five minutes, round the clock. The ATC system also assisted lost aircraft. Some of these changes were in effect by June and tonnage rates began rising again.

The extra tonnage was needed. The B-29s were becoming operational, and the Twentieth Air Force, to which they were assigned, became operational in April. Under a plan code-named *Matterhorn*, B-29s were to operate from China, in bases close enough for the bombers to reach Japan. All B-29s were assigned to the Twentieth Air Force. It operated independently of theater commanders or regionally assigned Air Forces, including the Tenth in India and the Fourteenth in China. Plans called for 100 B-29s operating out of China in March 1944 and 300 by September. They required dedicated airfields with reinforced runways long enough for the big bombers to operate from, and capable of taking the weight of the B-29s. B-29 base construction started the previous year.

B-29 production ran behind schedule. Instead of an operational wing of 100 B-29s by March, the first Superfortresses began arriving in India in April, in considerably smaller totals than originally envisioned. This was just as well. Construction on B-29 airfields in China and India was also behind schedule, too. They could not handle 100 B-29s by April 1944 and never were expanded to support 300.

OPPOSITE OPERATION *MATTERHORN*

B-29s taxi to lift off from Chengtu airfields at the beginning of the first mission to bomb the Japanese Home Islands. They flew up from Indian airfields, refueling at Chengtu before flying to Japan. This raid, on the Yawata steelworks, required bases in China to reach Kyushu. (AC)

Due to the vulnerability of airfields in China, the B-29s were based in India, at Bengal airfields west and north of Calcutta. They were too far from Japanese airfields in Burma to be attacked easily. The bombers were housed and maintained in India. From Bengal airfields, the B-29s could strike targets anywhere in French Indochina, Thailand, Malaya, and parts of the Dutch East Indies.

To attack targets in China, Manchukuo, Formosa, or Japan, they flew from airfields around Chengtu in Sichuan Province, in southwest China. Typically planes armed up in India, flew 1,200 miles from Bengal to Sichuan, refueled at the Chengtu airfields, and then flew to hit targets as far away as Kyushu. When the mission ended, they returned to Chengtu, refueled, and flew to their bases in India. Each combat sortie – sending one B-29 over a target in Manchukuo, Japan, or Formosa – required eight flights from India to China and back carrying fuel. Additional flights were required to carry supplies for the Chinese airfields supporting *Matterhorn*.

The Hump tonnage carried to support the Twentieth Air Force grew from 427 tons in February 1944 to 4,581 tons in September 1944. The latter figure exceeded the total monthly tonnage carried to China through August 1943, a year earlier. The ICD carried much of this, especially early on, but could not move all of it. Once the B-29s began bombing targets accessible only through Chinese airfields, one-third to one-half the total fuel used on these missions was carried to China by B-29s ferrying fuel between India and China. More was carried by a fleet of C-46s and C-109s assigned to the Twentieth Air Force. At its height, one-quarter of the tonnage flown to China supported the Twentieth Air Force.

China-based B-29s were proving unnecessary by late 1944. Even as development of the B-29 and the infrastructure to support B-29 operations in China stalled, the US drive across the Pacific accelerated. On the same day the Twentieth Air Force launched its first attack on the Japanese Home Islands, June 15, 1944, US Marines landed on the Marianas. The Marianas were closer to Japan than the Chengtu airfields and significantly closer to the US. They were also safer from Japanese attack. The Japanese Army in China was threatening an offensive to bring the Chengtu airfields within range of Japanese warplanes.

Upon capture of the Marianas, B-29 bases were built there. By November, B-29s were bombing Tokyo from the Marianas. Rather than reinforce a faltering Chinese operation, the USAAF shut it down. By March 1945, the last B-29 mission from China and India

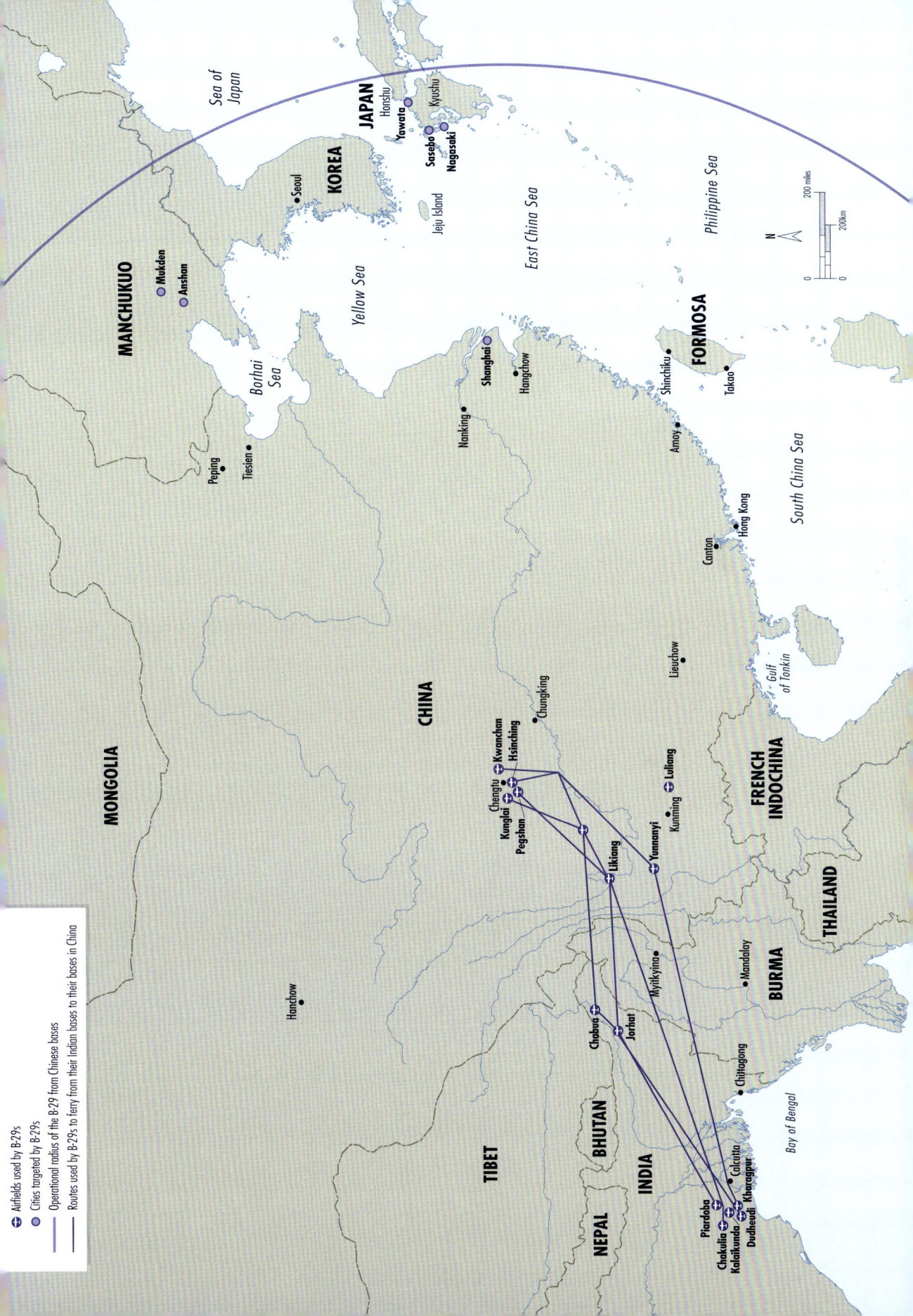

General William Tunner relieved Thomas Hardin in October 1944. Tunner was another transportation expert. After Hardin transformed the China airlift into a success, Tunner guided it as it evolved into a major airline, emphasizing efficiency and tonnage. This shows Tunner in Washington, prior to his service in the CBI. (Wikipedia)

was flown. Only 25 missions originated from the Chengtu airfields. By May the 58th Very Heavy Bombardment Wing, formerly stationed in Bengal and Sichuan, were attacking targets in Japan from Marianas bases.

Thomas Hardin departed the ICD as September 1944 ended, replaced by General William Tunner. This was not due to dissatisfaction with Hardin by Washington. Hardin transformed the airlift into an effective delivery system. He had been overseas a long time, and tiring. It was time to rotate him home.

Tunner, his replacement, was one of the most experienced airlift officers in the USAAF. He helped organize Ferry Command in 1941. He brought a seasoned cadre with him to run his headquarters, and lay down realistic plans to lift 100,000 tons each month.

1944 also saw the reopening of an overland route to China. Since June 1942, when he walked from Myitkyina to Ledo after Myitkyina's capture by the Japanese, Stilwell had insisted the key to victory was to reopen the Burma Road. He had not believed then, and did not believe in 1944, an airlift could move as many supplies as a truck route. He wanted an offensive to retake Upper Burma to provide access to the Burma Road, and to build a new road from Ledo, India to the Burma Road.

In 1942, when Washington initially made its strategic plans, this seemed the surest way forward. The airlift was then untried. No one seriously believed an airlift could move the tonnage it eventually did. Washington thought a road route necessary. The offensive was authorized, first for 1943. As with everything in the CBI, it was delayed a year, to 1944.

Stilwell convinced Chiang to allow the US Army to train Chinese divisions which would be used to retake Upper Burma. Chiang, wanting the US-trained troops, agreed, providing several divisions. He even gave permission to train the troops in India. The US would feed, house, and outfit these soldiers, relieving China of their logistical burden. In exchange Chiang got a body of well-trained soldiers. Through much of 1943, instead of returning to China empty, airlift transports carried Chinese infantrymen to India for training.

These flights proved difficult. The soldiers were all conscripts, typically farmers seized for the purpose. Many had never traveled in a motorized vehicle, much less flown in an airplane. They were unwilling and terrified. Some attempted to escape the army by jumping from the airplane. On several occasions, a panicked crush to escape through the rear doors when a plane started its takeoff run shifted the center-of-gravity aft enough to cause the transport to stall and crash on takeoff. Once aloft, sometimes the reluctant passengers became unruly. When this happened, the pilots took the unpressurized airplane high enough that the soldiers passed out from lack of oxygen.

Through 1943 and into the first months of 1944, Chiang refused to commit these troops to combat, no matter how ready they were. He planned to rely on them to defeat the Communists once the war with Japan ended. *U-Go* forced his hand. To relieve pressure on the British in India, he permitted Stilwell to use them in an offensive in Upper Burma.

A US force, the 5023rd Composite Group, known as "Merrill's Marauders," trained using Chindit tactics. Using infiltration tactics, they captured the airfield at Myitkyina. The Chinese divisions and heavy weapons were then flown in. By May 1944, Myitkyina's airfield was in Allied hands, and Myitkyina besieged. It fell in August. A second offensive from Yunnan pushed in to Burma along the path of the old Burma Road. By October, the Allies controlled territory for a new road route to China. Once the *U-Go* forces were in retreat, the British Army, commanded by General William Slim, pursued. By January 1945, the Allies controlled half of Upper Burma.

Allied control of this portion of Upper Burma permitted completion of the final section of the Ledo Road, running from Myitkyina to Loiwing, where it linked up with the old Burma Road. US Army engineers, largely from segregated Colored Construction Battalions, carved a two-lane graveled road from Ledo to Bhamo. It cut through some of the world's roughest terrain: mountainous, stream-divided jungle. Equally important, a six-inch petroleum pipeline paralleled it, reaching Myitkyina soon after the route from India to the town was cleared of Japanese interference.

One of the biggest benefits of reopening the Burma Road lay in what was beside it: a six-inch fuel pipeline from Ledo to Myitkyina and a four-inch fuel pipeline which ran to Kunming. The Kunming line supplied 3,150 tons (nearly 1 million gallons) of aviation fuel each month. (AC)

The Allies expanded the Myitkyina airfield, paving the runway, adding navigation beacons and landing lights. It was capable of taking large aircraft (including the four-engine C-54), and supporting night operations. It became so busy as a transportation hub, a second airfield was built at Myitkyina to relieve overcrowding. Additional satellite airfields were built throughout Upper Burma as the Allies advanced.

In what became a standard procedure, a field was hacked out by hand capable of landing transports or gliders. Small bulldozers were landed first. Engineers used these to quickly expand the airfield to a size where C-47s and C-46s could comfortably take off and land. These then moved materials and equipment to turn it into a functioning airfield. It became quicker and easier to supply forces in Burma by air than through the Ledo Road.

One major benefit of the capture of Myitkyina was that monthly tonnage to China soared. From June to November, tonnage grew from 16,000 tons to 35,000 tons per month. This despite transports now supplying troops in Burma. There were several reasons. The most important was the reduction of the threat offered by the IJA Air Force. Airlift transports could safely use the direct route from Assam to Kunming without fear of attack by the IJAAF. The route was shorter and required lower altitudes.

Moreover, emergency fields offered alternatives to bailing out over jungles if mechanical problems or fuel shortages made it impossible to reach Assam or China. The lower altitudes reduced the icing threat. They also allowed pilots to fly at altitudes where they could smoke without requiring oxygen. Smoking was almost universal among pilots. Since smoking was impossible while wearing an oxygen mask, many pilots skipped using oxygen, preferring tobacco. Many argued if there was enough oxygen to keep a cigarette burning, there was enough to allow them to fly safely.

The more southerly routes finally permitted the use of C-54s in the airlift, especially during the last quarter of 1944. They first appeared in early October 1944. The big planes could not fly over Upper Burma, where they never needed to fly higher than 15,000ft. Each C-54 carried twice the load of a C-46. There were never that many C-54s. Only 38 were assigned to the ICD by the end of 1945. The massive tonnage they carried made a big difference, regardless. As 1944 ended, the ICD was achieving monthly tonnage rates undreamed of when the airlift started.

OPPOSITE OPERATIONS *GRUBWORM* AND *COTTON TAIL*

By fall 1944, with Upper Burma north of Bhamo in Allied hands, flying C-54s on the China airlift became practical. This route had maximum elevations below 10,000ft. The absence of the Japanese air forces on this route permitted C-54s, considered strategic assets not to be risked in combat, to be used. (LOC)

The final war months: December 1944 to August 1945

The ICD was ready to flex its muscles in ways it never had before. Starting in December, it began massive airlifts of troops. It had been used for airdrops and airlifts of troops to Burma previously, but these were regimental or brigade-level movements, 3,000 to 4,000 men and their equipment. Now plans were underway to move up to 100,000 men and their equipment into and around China. The three airlift operations were codenamed *Alpha*, *Cotton Tail*, and *Grubworm*.

After the Marianas fell, Japan needed the troops in China to protect their now-vulnerable Home Islands. They attempted something previously unthinkable to the IJA: to end the Second Sino-Japanese War. Japan offered a retreat to the 1937 borders in exchange for Chinese neutrality towards Japan. If China had the Western Allies withdraw all military forces from China, Japan would withdraw their own from the portions of China it then held. A treaty of friendship would be negotiated on the basis of national equality. China could determine the status of Inner Mongolia and regain Hong Kong.

Chiang might have accepted these terms in 1942 or 1943. By October 1944, the US started reconquering the Philippines. Chiang knew Japan was doomed. He could wait out the inevitable Allied victory. Chiang demanded the return of Manchuria in addition to everything else Japan offered. The Japanese were unwilling to cede Manchukuo, previously annexed into Japan.

The Japanese could move anywhere into China they desired, although that meant yielding territory elsewhere. But the real threat China posed to Japan was the Fourteenth Air Force. Its aircraft could reach the Chinese coast and into the South China Sea, disrupting Japanese communications with their supply lines to Malay and the Dutch East Indies. The Fourteenth Air Force required fixed airfields to operate from, with significant permanent maintenance and logistical facilities. When the peace negotiations failed, the IJA launched a major ground offensive in late 1944 to capture these airfields.

The IJA did not need to hold captured airfields. Razing them and destroying the fixed facilities there, rendered them useless until they were rebuilt. The Twentieth Air Force fields in

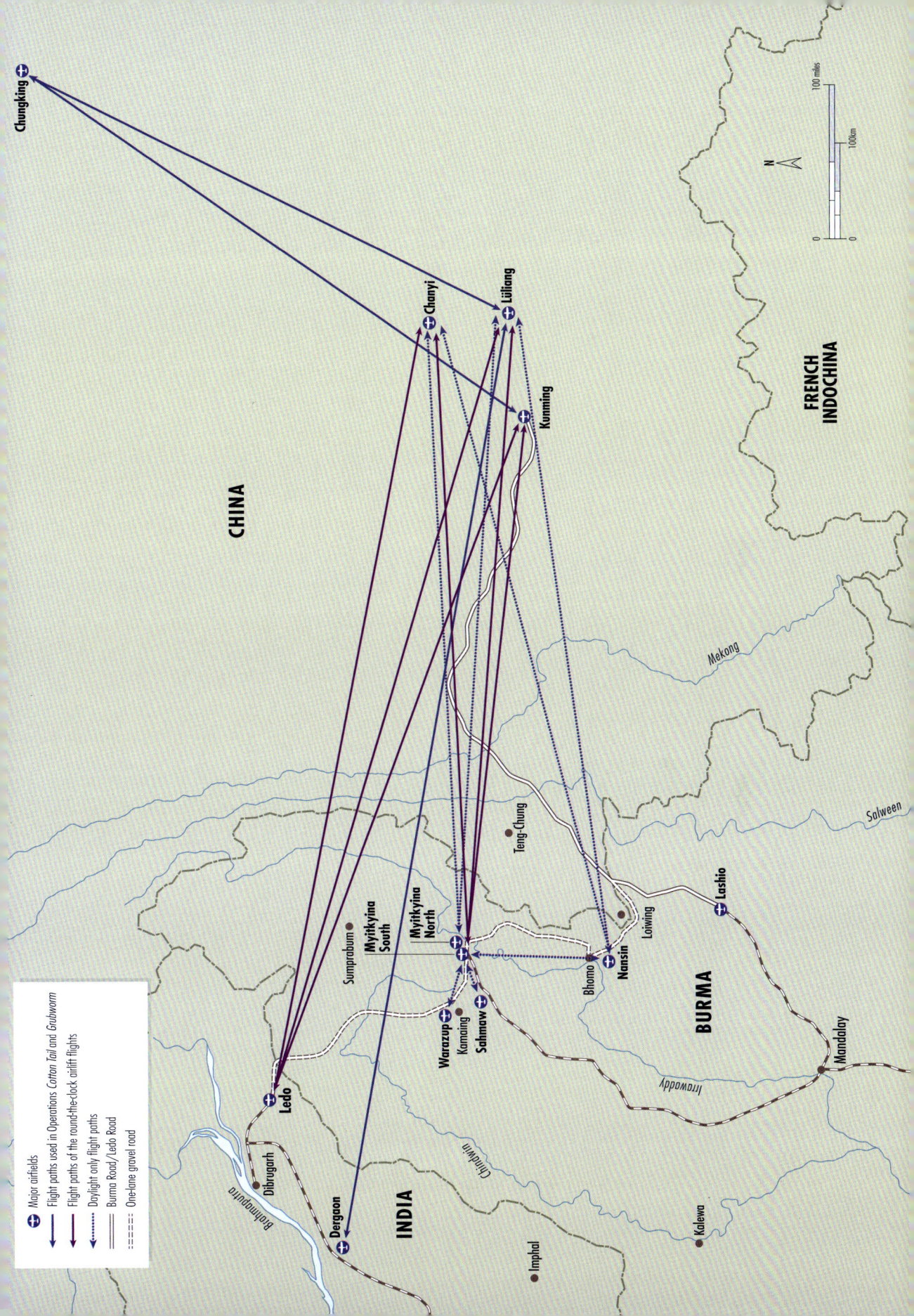

In January the ICD started publishing a weekly newspaper: *The Hump Express*. It emulated stateside newspapers. The front page contained news stories about flying the Hump, and the interior carried everything from advice columns to comics. This is the masthead of an early issue, published February 15, 1945. (AC)

Chengtu were too far from Japanese lines to be reached immediately, but the Fourteenth Air Force bases were within reach. The Japanese launched a major offensive in Guizhou Province.

Guizhou bordered Yunnan (with Kunming and Yunnanyi) and Sichuan (with the Chinese capital, Chungking). Its capture by Japan threatened both Kunming and communications between Kunming and Chungking. The Japanese were suffering supply problems as they moved into Guizhou, but the US did not know that. The Japanese commander had orders to stop after capturing the US airfields but made the Chinese believe his goal was Kunming. If stopped before that, he would still have achieved his objectives.

The Chinese lacked the local troops to stop the Japanese. They had a significant body of US-trained Chinese troops in Burma and troops available elsewhere in China. The US, after achieving its goals in Upper Burma, no longer needed the Chinese troops there. Chiang was unwilling to release them to aid the British elsewhere in Burma. The ICD had the resources to fly them to China, potentially as far as the US Fourteenth Air Force fields in Guizhou.

The US commander in China was General Albert Wedemeyer. He replaced Stilwell after Stilwell's relief on October 19, 1944. (Stilwell had irritated Chiang badly enough that Stilwell's removal was politically necessary.) Wedemeyer convinced Washington to approve the troop movements.

The massive airlift required cooperation between the ICD, the Tenth Air Force, and the Fourteenth Air Force. The move reduced supplies carried to the Fourteenth Air Force by 6,600 tons. The transports normally carrying those supplies would be carrying Chinese soldiers, instead. Transports from the Tenth Air Force were also required to generate the necessary lift from Burma to China.

On December 4, Operation *Alpha* began. This transferred 18,000 Chinese troops over 200 miles from Xian in Northern Shaanxi Province to Chanyi airfield in Northeastern Yunnan. From there, the troops moved into Guizhou. Troops were also sent from Chungking to Baoshan, but this movement was halted after 1,500 soldiers deserted at Yunnanyi, where the aircraft landed.

On December 13, the ICD portion of the airlift executed *Cotton Tail*. This involved moving 12,000 soldiers from Myitkyina to Chanyi. Chinese troops were taken by air from smaller airfields in Burma to Myitkyina and flown to China. The Tenth Air Force concurrently executed the rest of the lift, taking 14,000 soldiers and 1,600 horses from Burma to China. These troops were US-trained, and better motivated than those within China. The whole operation was called *Grubworm*.

Horses proved especially challenging. They were loaded into C-47s. The C-47s were partitioned into "stalls" created from bamboo poles to which the horses' halters were tied. The aircraft's floor was covered with 200lbs of straw and hay, spread to soak up the urine and manure. Four or five small horses were carried on each trip. The flights went surprisingly well. Only one horse broke free during the airlift. Crews preferred carrying horses to troops. The airlift ended January 5, 1945.

As it proved, the troops were not needed. The Japanese offensive culminated after taking the Guizhou airfields. These troop lifts were the first of several conducted within China. Aerial movement of troops by air became an important secondary role for US air power in China. Several multi-division troop airlifts were conducted in subsequent months.

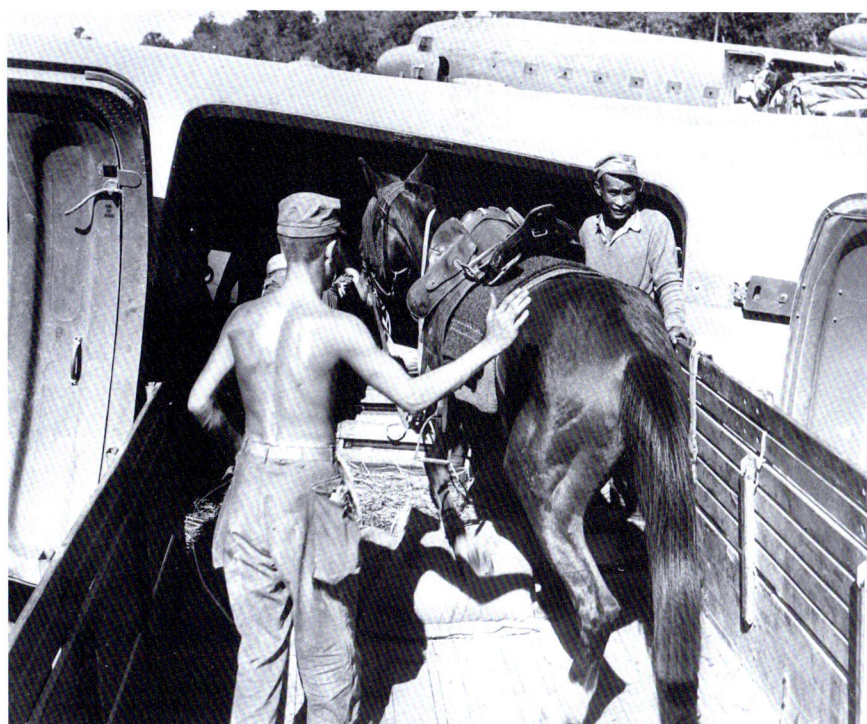

December 1944 saw the start of a series of mass movements of Chinese troops by air. These units used pack horses, which also had to be moved. Here a horse is being loaded into a Skytrain converted to carry horses. C-47s moved 1,600 horses during *Cotton Tail*. (AC)

The next day began what would later be known as "Black Week." Weather over the Hump had always been difficult. But this was a massive storm of unprecedented severity. It swept through Northern Burma and Southeastern China on January 6–7. Aircraft encountered updrafts of 60mph and headwinds, tailwinds, and crosswinds of 90 to 100mph. Aircraft flying through it, even large transports, were tossed about as if they were toys. Airspeeds abruptly changed from 300mph to 40mph and back. Aircraft gained or dropped thousands of feet of altitude within seconds. Hail and icing was reported from 15,000ft to 38,000ft – in a region with 16,000ft peaks.

The severe weather was on the eastern half of the flight, starting over Burma and continuing over China. Assam was unaware of its full force, and pilots arriving at Kunming were expected to fuel up and return regardless of weather. Some complied; others refused or declared mechanical emergencies. Finally at 10:30am on January 6, permission was given to stand down. Reports of losses that night ranged from 33 aircraft lost and 120 killed to an official total of nine ICD aircraft crashed and 31 dead. CNAC lost three aircraft and the Tenth and Fourteenth Air Forces another three. It was the worst single-night loss during the war.

Yet the ICD recovered quickly. Since assuming command, Tunner worked to improve morale and increase professionalism of ICD personnel. Part of it involved restoring military discipline and courtesy. Morning staff meetings became routine, airfield appearance was improved. Standards for personal grooming by ICD air and ground crew were upgraded. So were cockpit standards.

Tunner also began gathering statistics. How many hours were aircrew flying? Where were crashes most common? Where were the bottlenecks occurring? Answers were used to reduce accidents and crew fatigue and to increase the ICD's carrying capacity. Tunner was determined to turn the airlift into an airline operation, especially as the combat threat receded. Risks faced were more similar to those experienced by civilian airline operations than front-line combat air units.

Tunner also improved living conditions. Mess halls, operations rooms, theater, and athletic facilities were improved. He worked to foster unit pride, something previously neglected in the rush to build up the airlift. By fall 1944, airfield construction was mature. Attention could be focused on aesthetics. Tunner made public relations a priority, filling his command with posters and circulars to improve morale. *The Hump Express*, a weekly newspaper, began publication January 18, 1945.

It mimicked stateside newspapers. It had a page-one banner. There were front-page news stories, features highlighting ICD performance, photographic essays, pinup girls, local cartoons, even comic strips published stateside. The only thing missing was a classified advertising section.

The airlift matured by 1945. In January, the ICD had 375 airlift aircraft assigned to the China flights. The total bounced between 375 and 425 through the rest of the war, averaging 400 each month. The formerly ubiquitous C-47 had been largely replaced. There were only ten to 25 still on Hump runs. It had been largely superseded by the C-46, of which 150 to 180 were flying the route. The rest were four-engine aircraft, the C-87/C-109 and the C-54.

There were never more than 100 C-54s, but they were carrying nearly half the cargoes at the war's end. They operated from the Bengal airfields formerly used by Twentieth Air Force B-29s. These bases were available following the relocation of the 58th Wing to the Marianas, and were close to Calcutta. It had become a major cargo port as the Japanese threat to maritime traffic diminished. The straight-line path from these airfields to Kunming had the lowest flight altitude requirements of any path to China.

To deal with increased numbers of aircraft to maintain, Tunner introduced Product Line Maintenance. It was designed to enable high maintenance traffic with limited skilled personnel. Under the crew chief system, each aircraft was assigned a crew chief, a skilled engineer capable of conducting all maintenance on an aircraft, supervising what work he delegated to others. This worked well on advanced bases with limited resources and relatively few aircraft.

Maintaining the crew chief system in an environment with nearly 400 aircraft required as many highly skilled mechanics as aircraft. Since the ICD was at the far end of the world from the US, it was hard to find crew chiefs in sufficient numbers. It also meant some skills went underused, because some items, although done routinely, were done infrequently. Often these were critical, yet a crew chief's skills might be rusty due to the length of time since the last time he had performed the servicing.

By 1945 Kunming's airport was as crowded as any major airport in the United States. Aircraft arrived and departed at five-minute intervals. Weather permitting, operations continued 24 hours a day. Air Traffic Control was as sophisticated as at any big-city US airport. (AC)

PCM centralized maintenance. As they needed servicing, aircraft passed through seven specialized maintenance stations, each focused on a specific task. One serviced engines exclusively, a second maintained hydraulic systems, another looked after instruments, and down the line until all an aircraft's needs were serviced. It required fewer highly skilled mechanics and allowed mechanics to become expert at critical, specialized work. By March's end, PCM was in place and quality of maintenance improved.

Tunner also dealt with the issue of pilot shortages and crew rotation. From its beginning, there were issues with too few aircrew flying the Hump, and fatigue of those who did fly it. Pilot burnout limited capacity. Recognizing this, commanders rotated aircrew from Hump routes to easier trans-India routes and finally back Stateside after they had flown sufficient hours.

In the early days, the rotation policy actually worsened fatigue problems. Senior pilots, anxious to get home, seized every opportunity to fly to return home early. They flew impossible schedules, sometimes making daily flights to rack up several hundred hours in a month. Many failed to complete their tours, killed due to fatigue-caused errors, taking a valuable aircraft with them.

With more pilots available by 1945, and more experienced pilots, Tunner instituted new rotation policies. He kept the old requirement to fly 750 hours before being eligible for rotation, but shortened the time before rotation from one year to ten months. Pilots in theater ten months returned home, even without flying 750 hours. He also instituted a policy of permitting ground personnel to rotate out after two years in the CBI. There were few postings as arduous as the Hump. A rotation to Europe or Australia was attractive, even if you did not get back to the States.

By April 1945, the ICD was running virtually like an airline. Air Traffic Control managed dozens of flights concurrently throughout a day. There were schedules, trunk lines, and

The ATC in the CBI had evolved into the world's largest airline by 1945. This chart shows the major routes flown at war's end in August 1945. The ICD had trunk routes, feeder routes, and regular flight schedules by early January, as complex as a major US civilian airline.(AC)

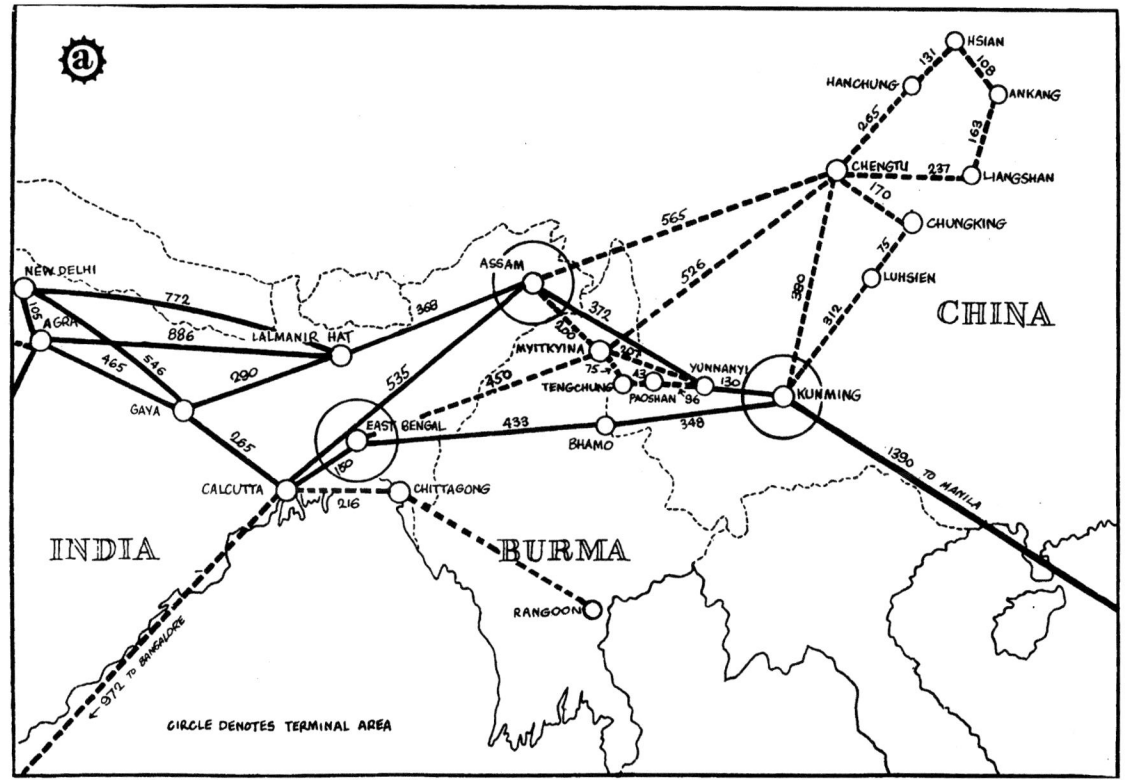

The first truck convoy to travel the Stilwell Road departed Ledo, India on January 12, 1945 and arrived at Kunming, China on February 4, three weeks later. Two-lane until it met the old Burma Road at Liuchow, it was single lane thereafter. Trucks driving to China stayed rather than returning. (AC)

feeder lines. Navigation aids available were on par with those in the US. On some routes the equivalent of stewardesses checked passengers in and looked after them during flights, including providing drinks. Only meal service was missing. It was impractical due to food spoilage due to the extreme heat.

Tonnage soared. By July the last full month of the war, the ICD shipped 71,000 tons to China. Forecasts of 100,000 tons per month by January 1946 were projected and being planned for. Tunner issued a challenge to see how many tons could be carried in one day for August 1, "Army Air Force Day." A remarkable 5,327 tons was carried that day. Despite the opening of the Stilwell Road (as Chiang ironically renamed the Ledo Road with Stilwell's departure), and the completion of a fuel pipeline from Calcutta to Kunming, the airlift remained China's primary supply line.

The first overland trip from Ledo to Kunming started January 12, 1945. On January 20, 1945, three vehicles from it reached Kunming. The rest arrived on February 4. Traffic was one-way from Bhamo to Kunming, so the vehicles were part of the goods delivered. Over the next eight months, the Stilwell Road brought 129,000 tons of supplies (which included the trucks carrying goods – it was a one-way trip) into China, an average of 18,500 tons per month.

Winding down – September 1945 to December 1945

The Pacific War ended on August 15, 1945 with Japan's surrender. Victory eliminated the purpose of the China airlift. There was no military reason to remain in China after Japan's surrender. Harry Truman replaced Franklin Roosevelt as US President after Roosevelt's April 1945 death. Truman lacked the emotional connection to China Roosevelt had, and had no grand plan to place China (presumably grateful to the US for its World War II assistance) as the US regional partner in Asia.

To Truman, the China-Burma-India Theater was one more distant place where the US was no longer needed. It was more distant and less important than most. It was time to go home. This did not immediately eliminate the need for the ICD or the US aerial presence in

Following the end of World War II, the Kuomintang government needed to reassert control over Japanese-held territory, often far distant from the front lines. The ATC flew 81,000 Chinese soldiers and their equipment from Kuomintang-held territory to Shanghai, Nanking, and Peking. This sped up Kuomintang control of these areas. (AC)

China. Shipments to China continued to support a US withdrawal, although they continued at a slower pace.

Tunner began stressing safety over tonnage. The war was over. Spacing between flights increased to reduce accident risk, especially midair collisions. Pilots had to fly by instrument flight rules. The C-87s were limited to daytime flying. Most cargo traveled on C-46, which by September 1945 was a well-tested and reliable aircraft. Only experienced pilots commanded passenger flights, with newcomers and less-stellar performers limited to cargo carrying. Pilots were limited to 100 hours of flight time per month, roughly one round-trip flight from Assam to China every other day.

The ICD had three principal responsibilities in the immediate postwar months: to continue supplying US forces in China, to support the draw-down of US personnel in China, and to assist the Chinese to occupy formerly Japanese-held regions of China.

The first was the most important, but along with the third responsibility, unpopular. It kept air and ground crew in China and India when their only desire was to head home.

It was absolutely necessary as the supply flights carried the fuel and supplies necessary to conduct the other missions with which the airlift was tasked. Pilots especially resented taking non-essential goods for Chinese senior leaders, feeling they were risking lives carrying luxuries for Chinese generals and politicians.

These flights continued three full months after the war's end, officially terminating on November 15, 1945. While they did not match the tonnage carried prior to August 15, it was still substantial. Approximately 75,000 tons of supplies were carried between August 15 and November 15. Much of what was carried was fuel, since the fuel pipeline ended in Kunming and air operations continued throughout China.

A complex problem involved moving Chinese troops to Japanese-held areas. Japan had roughly 600,000 soldiers in China when it surrendered. While some were facing the Soviets, the Kuomintang had to accept the surrender of at least two-thirds of these troops, disarm them, and repatriate them to Japan. Complicating the operation was that with the end of the war with Japan, the Kuomintang and Communist factions in China were beginning a civil war to determine which would control China. (In some regions, the Kuomintang did not disarm Japanese troops, using them as co-belligerents against a common Communist foe.)

The US wanted Japanese forces removed from China, and Chinese control established over previously Japanese-occupied portions of China. The US wanted this done as expeditiously as possible, to prevent China from collapsing into chaos. Washington did not wish US involvement in a Chinese civil war, viewing it as a domestic issue, outside US interests.

The US agreed to transport Kuomintang troops by air to major cities, to ensure speedy Chinese reoccupation of the major ports. The biggest operation moved 26,000 troops of the Chinese 94th Army from Luichow to Shanghai. This was approximately 900 miles, and complicated by a lack of aviation fuel once aircraft left Indian airfields. Because of the size of the movement, C-54s were used exclusively.

The Skymasters were loaded with fuel drums at their Bengal airfields, and flew to Luichow 1,200 miles away. They offloaded the fuel at Luichow, loaded enough fuel for the 1,800-mile

A Chinese soldier stands sentry at a US airfield in China in December 1945. By then the Hump airlift had officially ended and the US was withdrawing their forces that still remained in China. The airfields from which the US operated and anything left behind were turned over to the Chinese. (AC)

round trip from Luichow to Shanghai and back, and flew a load of Chinese troops to Shanghai. They refueled at Luichow, and returned to Bengal, to repeat the cycle after a layover in India. A round trip involved 23 hours in the air, plus four to six hours on the ground at each of the three stops.

Additional movements flew 95th Army troops to Peking and Nanking. The troop lifts were conducted in two waves, between September 6 and October 27. In addition to the 26,000 soldiers and their equipment moved to Shanghai, the Bengal Wing of the ACD moved 81,000 other Chinese troops within China. This permitted Chiang and the Kuomintang to reassert control over China in weeks, rather than the months required had the armies moved by foot.

The ICD also was an instrument of demobilization. There were tens of thousands of US soldiers in China, Burma, and India when the war ended. These were brought home over the next few months. The quickest way to repatriate them was to fly them to embarkation ports where they could board ships headed stateside.

Aircraft headed to Karachi from Assam airfields carried homeward-bound personnel with them, before loading with supplies for the return trip. Called Operation *Hope*, it carried 14,000 servicemen and women. US personnel in China were flown to Chinese ports. There they boarded ships heading to America's Pacific Coast. Some traveled aboard US Navy warships converted to troop carriers, part of Operation *Magic Carpet*. A lucky few, mostly aircrew or US Army Air Force personnel, flew home on US-bound ATC transports or returning stateside as part of the withdrawal.

Among those headed home was General Tunner. His wife was to undergo brain surgery. Arnold relieved Tunner in late October so he could be with her. He turned over command of the ICD to Brigadier General Charles Lawrence, the ICD's last commander. The ICD formally terminated its activities in China on November 15, 1945, bringing the curtain down on the Hump airlift.

AFTERMATH AND ANALYSIS

A line of US Air Force and US Navy transports unload cargo at Berlin's Tempelhof Airport during the 1948–49 Berlin airlift. A Hump alumnus, William Tunner ran the Berlin airlift and some of the other Berlin airlift participants had flown the Hump in World War II. (Wikipedia)

The US Army Air Force remained in China for a few months after the official termination of the airlift, but this was completing the withdrawal of the US from China. China was sliding into civil war; the US was uninterested in participating. Eventually the Kuomintang government would lose to the Communists, fleeing the mainland.

The Kuomintang hung onto a few offshore islands (most notably Matsu and Amoy) and Formosa, which reverted to its Chinese name, Taiwan. There they remained, awaiting an opportunity to return to the mainland that never came. They retain a precarious independence that continues to the present, despite Communist China's threats to reestablish control of Taiwan by invasion.

Over the next 70 years, China achieved half of Roosevelt's vision. They became the major power in Eastern Asia and the surrounding waters. The other half crumbled to dust. Instead of an ally following the leadership of the US, China has become the US's principal strategic adversary in the Far East. It eclipsed Russia as the US's main global rival in the 21st century.

This was one political upheaval shaking Asia in the immediate postwar years. India, Burma, and Malaya all gained independence. Burma is now Myanmar. Singapore established itself as a city-state independent of the rest of what became Malaysia. British India partitioned into India and Pakistan in 1947. Bangladesh split from Pakistan in 1971. Assam became part of India; the portions of Bengal where the Twentieth Air Force (and later C-54) airfields were located are now part of Bangladesh.

The airlift established a foundation of aerial global reach for the US Air Force, when it was established as an independent branch of the US military in 1947. Airlift was and remains a major role for the USAF. Transportation is less glamorous than strategic bombing or air superiority, but is vitally necessary for the fighting force to project itself. Military professionals assert, "Amateurs talk strategy and tactics; professionals talk logistics." The US airlift capability was the biggest in the world – and evolved from the China airlift.

The officers involved in the airlift generally went on to long, productive, and influential USAF careers. Three years after leaving China, William Tunner would run the ultimately successful Berlin airlift. Much of that success was due to lessons learned from the China airlift on the Hump route. He retired from the Air Force after a 32-year career. Alexander, Old, Hoag, and Hardin also moved into senior commands in the USAF, all retiring in the 1950s.

From April 1942 to November 1945, the Air Transport Command and its immediate predecessor, the Assam-Burma Command, carried 738,667 tons of supplies from India to China. Ninety percent of the tonnage was carried in 1944 and 1945, with 60 percent carried in 1945. The 1942 and 1943 totals were miniscule by comparison: 3,540 tons in 1942 and 51,103 tons in 1943.

The ATC also ferried 4,671 aircraft from the United States to China. The majority were transports, 1,438 of which went to the ATC, 977 to the numbered Air Force in China, and 103 to the Chinese government. The rest were warplanes, most of which went to the USAAF combat units, but 153 of which went to the Chinese. These totals only include aircraft flown from the US. Other aircraft, including Lend-Lease P-43s and P-66s, were shipped crated to Karachi and assembled in India.

Cargo totals exclude tonnage carried to China by CNAC or the Tenth, Fourteenth, and Twentieth Air Forces (except for the 1942 tonnage carried by the Assam-Burma Command when it was part of the Tenth Air Force).

CNAC carried 100 to 500 tons per month in 1942 and 1943, and up to several thousand tons per month by 1945. At least 75,000 tons were carried by CNAC over the course of the airlift. Its totals were tracked internally within CNAC. The exact numbers appear to have been lost during the chaos of the Chinese Civil War. Maintaining archives was not a high priority for CNAC management in those years.

Both the Tenth and Fourteenth Air Forces moved supplies to China when flights took them between China and India. A good example of this was missions the Fourteenth Air Force flew to counter the *Tsuzigiri* fighter sweeps. The B-24s offering themselves as Hayabusa bait moved both fuel and .50cal ammunition to China on each flight back to their home bases. The excess of both sustained combat operations in China, and the B-24 pilots took the opportunity to return to China with bomb bay auxiliary fuel tanks filled. Similarly aircraft ferried to China typically carried critical spare parts and extra fuel as the opportunity provided. These cargoes are not included in the ATC tonnage totals.

The Twentieth Air Force, while operating in China, maintained an independent transportation wing. The ATC provided only part of the supplies used by the Twentieth.

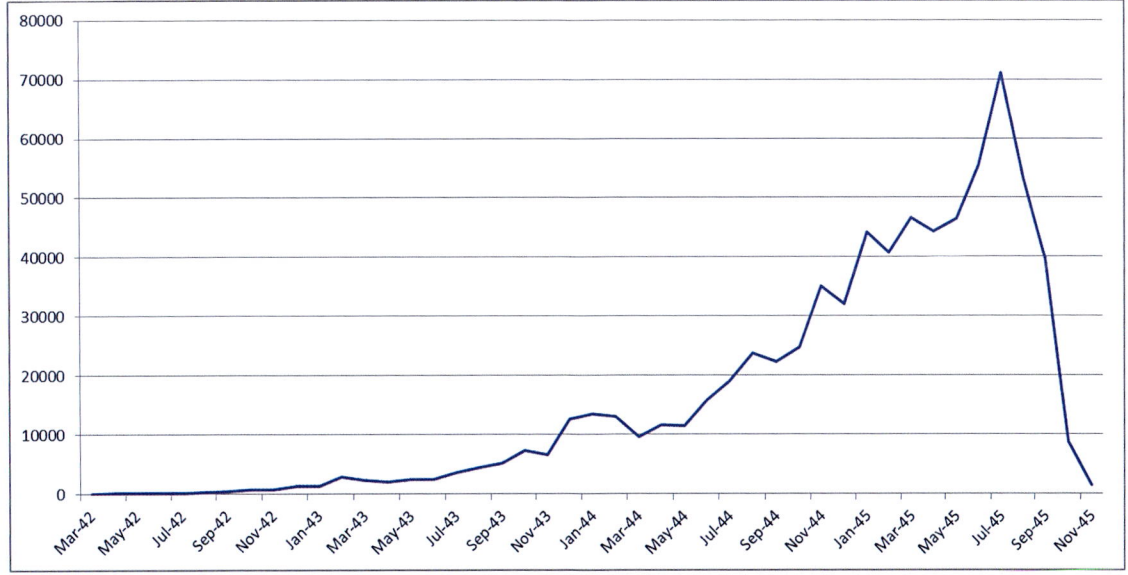

Tonnage flown to China by the India-China Division and its predecessor, the Assam-Burma Ferry Command between March 1932 and November 1945. This is only the tonnage carried by the ATC. These totals exclude tonnage carried by CNAC, and the Tenth, Fourteenth, and Twentieth Air Forces. (AC)

The rest was carried by the Twentieth, either by the B-29s flying missions or dedicated transports controlled by the Twentieth. The amount of supplies flown in by the Twentieth each month varied from 41 tons to 3,000 tons. (Most of what was carried by the Twentieth was fuel. The ATC carried most supplies needed to support the Twentieth's ground element.)

The Twentieth Air Force received its own fleet of C-109 tankers in September 1944. This was shortly before the decision to transfer the B-29s to the Marianas. When the Twentieth closed down operations in India, the C-109s and C-46s forming its transport wing were transferred to the ICD. Their tonnage thereafter counted towards the ATC total. This contributed to the tonnage jump seen in 1945.

Most of what was carried into China supported US forces in China, especially the Fourteenth Air Force and (after it redeployed to China) the Tenth Air Force. Of the 670,000 tons taken to China by the ATC, only 36,000 tons went to the Chinese government. The other 95 percent went to serve the needs of the Tenth and Fourteenth Air Forces and the ATC itself. This included fuel and ordinance. These were the largest fractions carried. Other large fractions included materials for building base facilities (including runways and hangars), and supplies and food to support US personnel in China.

Chiang was always less interested in receiving supplies to improve the Chinese Army than he was from seeing high levels of deliveries as a token of US commitment to China. He was also happy to leave fighting Japan to the US Army Air Force. Chiang willingly accepted any aid and training the US gave his troops, but intended to save those troops for the post-World War II confrontation expected with the Communists. He committed his own troops to combat against the Japanese only reluctantly, and only under absolute necessity to do so.

One-third of the supplies delivered to the Chinese were not war-related, especially in 1945. Three-quarters of what was shipped in 1944 was war-related, chiefly fuel, ordinance, and medical supplies. The rest was "miscellaneous." As 1945 started, and Japan's defeat became inevitable, deliveries of military stores ceased. Of the 6,547 tons delivered to the Chinese government in 1945, 97 percent was categorized as "miscellaneous." This consisted mostly of private goods and luxuries shipped to Chinese leaders. These included goods as varied as beer, prophylactics, a shrubbery (for a general's house), baled cloth, and ping-pong tables. Unnecessary for the war effort, it contributed to the reputation China had for corruption.

The cost was heavy. At least 594 aircraft were lost, including 468 US and 41 CNAC aircraft. Along with these, 1,314 air crewmen and passengers were killed flying the Hump. Another 345 others were missing, presumed dead, while flying aboard one of the 81 aircraft which vanished in the mountains or jungle and were never found. Another 1,200 aircrew or passengers survived bailout or crash. They were rescued or walked back to Allied lines on their own.

Whether the Hump airlift was a success depends upon how success is defined. It was a propaganda victory on several levels. During the darkest days of 1942, it seemed to offer some of the few seeming victories the US experienced. The AVG offered the only effective efforts against the Japanese in Burma in spring 1942. Although their victory claims were exaggerated, they outscored the Japanese. The Doolittle Raid required aerial resupply from India to China to be attempted.

In late 1942 and early 1943, China seemed to be the shortest road to Tokyo. That promise made the airlift worth attempting. By December 1943, when it was running at the scale needed for a China-based offensive, other more promising paths to victory emerged. China was no longer needed. By then it gained its own momentum, continuing to grow despite its diminishing strategic utility.

Nor was the airlift necessary to keep China in the war. Once the US entered the war, Chiang felt certain Japan's eventual defeat was inevitable. He just had to wait until the US inevitably defeated Japan to get all of China back. From the end of 1942 until the war ended, Japan offered Chiang increasingly favorable terms for China to conclude a separate peace

The China airlift cost nearly 600 aircraft and 1,650 dead or missing. Another 1,200 survived a crash or successfully bailed out. Some of those men, like this survivor being rescued from a tree, were injured. Rescue of downed aircrew and passengers became a priority in the last two years of the war. (AC)

with Japan. Chiang, determined to restore China to its pre-1931 borders, refused every offer knowing if he was a US ally when the war ended, he would get everything. His threats to make peace with Japan were negotiating ploys, a way to get more support from the US, and a means to be treated as a major partner instead of a suppliant ally.

Despite everything, the airlift yielded significant results. It became an increasingly powerful symbol of US air power. It was the testbed for aerial resupply and for aerial support of ground operations. This included resupply of ground troops behind enemy lines and even aerial evacuation of wounded.

Surviving aircraft

As with most Pacific War campaigns, there are many examples of surviving US aircraft types and a shortage of Japanese aircraft types. This is more than typically true of aircraft participating in the China airlift. The numbers of US aircraft participating were much greater than that of the Japanese. Not only were there far fewer Japanese aircraft, they were less likely to survive due to the total destruction of Japan's air forces by the end of the war.

The US aircraft were also more likely to survive postwar, due to their nature. Transports have significant peacetime utility in air forces and greater civilian application than do warbirds. Transports also become obsolete significantly slower than warbirds. Far fewer transports were sent straight to postwar scrapyards than their more warlike contemporaries.

The C-47/C-53 probably fared best. Several dozen are still flying commercially, although not in passenger service. There are at least 70 examples of various types of the military versions of the DC-3 on display in various museums and reenactment groups in the US alone. I cannot confirm whether any of these flew the Hump, but it is likely. There are even eight surviving DC-2s, although none appear to have flown for CNAC.

Over 50 C-46 Commandos still exist. Three are still in commercial service. There are five in China and one in Taiwan, all of which were likely to have flown the Hump. A C-46 forms a prominent part of the US Air Force Museum's Hump display.

I could not find any surviving examples of the unbeloved C-87 or C-109. The C-54 Skymaster fared better, but not much. There are five non-flying examples and "Spirit of Freedom," a flying example owned by the Berlin Airlift Historical Foundation in New Jersey. It operated in the Caribbean during World War II and participated in the Berlin airlift. The smaller C-47s and C-46s fared better because they were simpler and could operate from primitive airfields. There was more postwar demand for these as bush aircraft than there was for aircraft requiring paved runways.

There are six examples of Ki-43s still surviving and five reproduction Hayabusas. The reproductions are pieced together from different wrecks or have new parts fabricated to replace destroyed components. None are airworthy and several of the originals are unrestored. Some Ki-21s survived World War II. Some of these survived postwar after being converted into transports. None of these survived into the 21st century. There appear to be no surviving examples.

There appear to be three Ki-48s still surviving today. All are non-flyable and in museums. One is in China, one in Indonesia, and the third in Moscow, apparently seized during the period when the Soviet Union invaded Japanese-held China in August 1945.

A surviving Curtiss C-46 Commando forms the centerpiece of the Hump display now at the National Museum of the United States Air Force at Wright-Patterson Air Force Base in Dayton, Ohio. It also shows some of the cargoes carried. One cargo carried was metal planking used to build runways. (William Lardas)

FURTHER READING

Probably the best widely available book about the US airlift to China is John D. Plating's *The Hump: America's Strategy for Keeping China in World War II* (Texas A&M University Press, College Station, Texas, 2011). It is an expansion of his doctoral dissertation, which is available online. An excellent book, it goes into many of the personal and political aspects of the airlift that I excluded due to space limitations. Another first-rate account is Caroline Alexander's *Skies of Thunder: The Deadly World War II Mission Over the Roof of the World* (Viking, New York, New York, 2024). In addition to being a gripping account, it too covers the soft aspects of the campaign I had to neglect.

Other major sources include the official histories of the CBI printed postwar by the US Army and the US Air Force. These works provided much of the technical details I include. Also providing insight were the relevant reports of the US Strategic Bombing Survey. Compiled in the immediate postwar years, they reported on technical aspects of the air war. Most are now available online (as are the various official histories used). I also found accounts of the Japanese side of the war compiled by various services postwar. Books available online are marked with an "*" below.

Other principal sources used for this book are:

Craven, Wesley Frank and Cate, James Lea (editors), *The Army Air Forces In World War II, Volume One, Plans and Early Operations, January 1939 to August 1942*, Office of Air Force History, Washington, D.C., 1983*

Craven, Wesley Frank and Cate, James Lea (editors), *The Army Air Forces In World War II, Volume Four: The Pacific: Guadalcanal to Saipan, August 1942 to July 1944*, Office of Air Force History, Washington, D.C., 1983*

Craven, Wesley Frank and Cate, James Lea (editors), *The Army Air Forces In World War II, Volume Five: The Pacific: Matterhorn to Nagasaki, June 1944 to August 1945*, Office of Air Force History, Washington, D.C., 1983*

Francillon, René J., *Japanese Aircraft of the Pacific War*, Funk & Wagnalls, New York, NY, 1970

A memorial to the pilots and aircrew that flew the Hump in the China-Burma-India Theater during World War II was erected by the US Air Force. Located in Memorial Park at the National Museum of the United States Air Force in Dayton, Ohio, it commemorates all personnel participating in the China airlift. (NMAF)

Gann, Ernest K., *Fate is the Hunter*, Simon & Schuster, Inc., New York, New York, 1961

Headquarters, United States Army, Japan, *Burma Operations Record: 15th Army Operations in the Imphal Area and Withdrawal to Northern Burma*, Japanese Monograph 134, Japan, 1957

Romanus, Charles F. and Sunderland, Riley, *United States Army in World War II, The China-Burma-India Theater, Vol 1: Stilwell's Mission to China*, Center of Military History, Washington, D. C., 1953*

Romanus, Charles F. and Sunderland, Riley, *United States Army in World War II, The China-Burma-India Theater, Vol 2: Stilwell's Command Problems*, Center of Military History, Washington, D. C., 1956*

Romanus, Charles F. and Sunderland, Riley, *United States Army in World War II, The China-Burma-India Theater, Vol 3: Time Runs Out in CBI*, Center of Military History, Washington, D. C., 1959*

Tunner, Lt. Gen. William H., *Over the Hump*, Air Force History and Museums Program, Washington, D. C., 1998*

United States Strategic Bombing Survey, *Air Operations in China, Burma, India World War II*, Washington, D. C., 1947

United States Strategic Bombing Survey, *The Air Transport Command in the War Against Japan*, Washington, D. C., 1946

United States Strategic Bombing Survey, *The Strategic Air Operation of Very Heavy Bombardment in the War Against Japan (Twentieth Air Force)*, Washington, D. C., 1947*

United States Strategic Bombing Survey, *Japanese Air Power*, Washington, D. C., 1946*

United States Strategic Bombing Survey, *The Japanese Aircraft Industry*, Washington, D. C., 1947*

INDEX

Note: page numbers in bold refer to photographs, illustrations and captions.

ABC (Assam-Burma Command), the 51, 55, 57, 58, 89
accidents and crashes 11, **17,** 54, 55, 58, **59, 63, 65,** 65–68, **69,** 70, 73, 76, 81, 85, 90, **91**
   forced landings **13**(**14–15**), 69
ACD, the 87
air formations 32, **32**
air superiority 25
air tactics 31–32
aircraft 18, 24, 25, 51, 91–92
   Boeing B-17 (US) 34, 51
   Boeing B-29 Superfortress (US) 10, 17–18, 19, 34, 73–76, **74,** 82, 90
   Consolidated B-24 Liberator (US) 17, 34, **(65)66–67,** 68, 70, 89
   Consolidated C-87 Express (US) 10, **16, 46,** 58, **59, 65,** 68, 69, 82, 85, 92
   Consolidated C-109 Liberator (US) 10, 16, **16,** 21, 74, 82, 90, 92
   Curtiss C-46 Commando (US) 10, 11, 12, 16–17, **17,** 18, **42, 46,** 63, **64,** 68, 69, 70, **73, 74,** 77, 82, 85, 90, 92, **92**
   Curtiss P-40 Warhawk (US) 17, 27, 48, **49, 51,** 55, 56, 69, 70
   Douglas C-33 (US) 12, 13
   Douglas C-47 Skytrain (US) 10, **12,** 13, **13**(**14–15**), 18, **21, 33,** 36, **46,** 50, 51, **51**(**52–53**), 54, **54,** 55, 56, **56,** 58, 63, 64, **64,** 65–68, 70, 77, 80, **81,** 82, 92
   Douglas C-53 Skytrooper (US) 10, **12,** 13, 36, **51**(**52–53**), 56, 92
   Douglas C-54 Skymaster (US) 10, 17, **46,** 77, **78,** 82, 86–87, 88, 92
   Douglas DC-2/C-32 (US) 12, 13, 92
   Douglas DC-3 (US) **12,** 50, 92
   Kawasaki Ki-48 "Lily" (Japan) 25, 26–27, 38, **51**(**52–53**), 56, **57,** 92
   Mitsubishi Ki-15 "Babs" (Japan) 25
   Mitsubishi Ki-21 "Sally" "Gwen" (Japan) **24,** 25–26, **32, 51 (52–53),** 56, **57**
   Mitsubishi Ki-46 "Dinah" (Japan) 25, 56
   Nakajima Ki-27 "Nate" (Japan) 25, 39, **40**
   Nakajima Ki-43 Hayabusa "Oscar" (Japan) 25, **27,** 30, 31, 38, 39, **40, 51**(**52–53**), **55,** 56, **(65)66–67,** 68, **69,** 89, 92

   North American B-25 Mitchell (US) 17, 51–54, 65–68
   North American P-51 Mustang (US) 17
   Republic P-43 Lancer (US) 17, 54, **55,** 89
   Vultee P-66 Vanguard (US) 17, 54–55, 89
aircrew morale 56, 68, 77, 81, 85
aircrew shortages 63, 72, 83
airfields 9, **11,** 12, 18–19, 27, 32, **32,** 37, 40, 50–51, **(51)52–53, 57,** 64, 73, **74,** 78–80, **86**
   and living conditions 55, 82
Myitkyina **4,** 8, 9, 10, 21, 28, 33, 36, 38, 39, **40,** 41, 50, 51, 54, 68, 69, 76, 77, 80
airlift tactics 22
airportable bulldozers **64**
Alexander, Brig Gen Edward 58, 59, 63, 64, 89
Allied submarines **28,** 28–29
altitudes 16, 17, 19–20, **56,** 77, **78,** 81, 82
Arnold, Gen Henry "Hap" 36, 50, 51, 54, 55, 57, 59, 62, 63, 87
ATC (air traffic control) 73, 83–84, **85**
ATC (Air Transport Command), the 10, 22, 58, **58,** 59, 64, **83, 85,** 89, **89,** 90
AVG (American Volunteer Group), the 5, 32, 34, 48, 49, **49,** 59, 90

Battle of Kohima (April 1944), the 10
Berlin airlift, the **88,** 89, 92
Bissell, Brig Gen Clayton 58, 59–62
"blood chits" 9
bombloads 25, 26, **51**
Brereton, Maj Gen Lewis 50, 58
Bridge Over the River Kwai, The (novel) 29
British interests and actions 6, 8, 9, 12, 18, 27, 34, 37, 38, 48, 49, **61,** 62, 64, 72, 77
Burma Road, the **4,** 5–6, **6–7,** 8, 9, 19, 33, 36, 38, **39,** 45–48, **48,** 49, 50, 62, 68, 77
Burma-Thai Railroad, the 29, **29**

Cairo Conference, the **36,** 37, 70
Calcutta-Kunming fuel pipeline, the 70
cargo system, the 13, 16, **16,** 20, 45, 50, 63, **92**
   and tonnage shipped 10, 29, **34,** 36, **36,** 37, 39, 40, 45, **54,** 56, 57, 58, 59, 62, 63, 64, 65, **68,** 70, 72, 74, 76, **76,** 77, 84, 85–86, 89, **89,** 90
Casablanca Conference, the **58,** 62
CBI (China-Burma-India) Theater, the 33, **64, 72,** 84–85
CCP (Chinese Communist Party), the 43, 44

Chennault, Claire 37, 48, 59, 62, **65**
Chiang, Kai-Shek 4, 6, **36,** 37–38, 43, 44, 45, 54, 59, 62, 70, 76, 80, 84, 87, 90–91
China airlift, the 8, 10, 18, 33, **34,** 39, 42, 50, 58, **72,** 88, 90, 91, **91**
Chindits, the 19, 41, **70,** 70–72, 76
Chinese aims and priorities 34–36, 37–38, 76, 78, 80, 87, 90–91
Chinese civil conflict 4–5, 86, 88, 89
Churchill, Winston 62, 70
CNAC (China National Aviation Corporation) 6, 8, 9, 10, **33,** 36, 38, **50,** 57, 81, 89, 90, 92
Communist Chinese forces 4, 5, 37, 86, 88
conscripted manual labor **11, 18,** 19, **19,** 29, 55, 57
"cumulogranite" **13**(**14–15**)

deaths 10, 20, 29, **29, 57,** 81, 83, 90, **91**
dogfights 31, 56
Doolittle Raid, the 10, 51, 54, **54,** 90

elephant cargo cranes **73**
engineering capability 9, 18, 19, **19,** 38, 77, 82
engines 11, 13, 16, 17, 25, 26–27, 30, 31, 32, 55, 62, 82, 83
European colonial possessions 8, 38

fighter escorts 32
fighter sweeps 32, 56, **(65)66–67,** 68, 69, **69,** 89
Fisher, Col William **65**
flight paths **46–47**
flying fatigue 63, 83
Fort Hertz 21, 38, 55, 59, **60–61,** 68, 69
French Indochina 8, 9, 44, 48
fuel supplies 22, 29, 48, 51, **54, 65,** 69, 72, 89

Gann, Ernest 16, **16,** 17
George, Col Harold 57, 58, 62
German actions and strategy 5, 6, 9, 45, 48, 49
ground stations 22
Guizhou offensive, the 80

Hammell, "Ridge" **13**
Hardin, Col Thomas 10, 22, 64–65, **68, 69,** 70, 73, 76, **76,** 89
Hayes, Col Caleb B. 51
Hoag, Brig Gen Earl **64,** 73, 89
horses on airlifts 80, **81**
Hump Express, The (newspaper) **80,** 82

INDEX

ICD (India-China Division), the 10, 72–73, 74, 78, 80, **80**, 81, 82, 84, 85–86, 87
ice formation on aircraft **(13)14–15**, 16, **16**, 17, 19, 43, **46**, 55, 77, 81
ICW (India-China Wing), the 58, 59, 62, 64, **68**, 72
IJA (Imperial Japanese Army), the **4**, 24, **24**, 25, **27**, 39, 40, **43**, 48, 78–80, 86
Fifth Air Army 70
IJA Air Force (Imperial Japanese Army Air Force), the 24, 28, 31–32, 38, 40, **40**, 41, 55, 56, **57**, 68, **69**, 77
3rd Hikodishan 25, 27, **51**
50th Sentai **(65)66–67**, 68
chutai 31
IJN (Imperial Japanese Navy), the 24, 44
imperial China and collapse 43–44
indigenous tribes **13**, 20
interdiction missions 24, 28, 30, 40, 68

Japanese Home Islands, the 34, 72, 74, **74**, 78
Japanese occupation of Burma 27, 33, 49–50
Japanese strategy **4**, **6**, 8, 9, 10, 24, 27–30, 31–32, 33, 38–41, **39**, **40**, 48, 49, 51, **(51)52–53**, 54, 55–56, 68, **69**, 69–72, **70**, 74, 78, 80
leaflet drops 41
and surrender 84
jungle infiltration tactics 41, **70**, 70–71, 76

Kunming airport 82
Kuomintang Nationalist government and army, the 4–5, 34–36, 37, 43, 44, **45**, 76, 80, **85**, **86**, 86–87, 88, 90
Yoke Force 59, 62

Lawrence, Brig Gen Charles 87
Ledo (Stilwell) Road, the 19, **19**, 33, **37**, 70, 77, 84
logistics 12, 18, 28–30, 36, 42, 88
and supply lines 8, 28, **28**, 30, 33, **35**, 80
Luce, Henry 6

Manchukuo (Manchuria) 4, 78
Mao, Tse Tung 44
Marshall, Gen George C. 50
matériel losses **51(52–53)**, 56, 68, 69, 70, 81, 90
mechanical issues 16–17, 63
military production 5, 16, 25, 26, 27, 34, 54, 55, 63, 73
military strength 25, 30
Mishmi, the **13**
Molotov-Ribbbentrop Pact (1939), the 5
museum exhibits 92, **92**
muzzle velocities 21, 30, 31

Naiden, Brig Gen Earl 50–51
navigation systems **21**, 21–22, 54, 59, **61**, 84

homing beacons 40, 59, 68, 73, 77
Low-Frequency Radio Range Navigation **(22)23**
Radio Range stations 73
night flight missions 55, 70
North African theater, the 54

obsolescence 25, 26, 27, **40**, 48, 49, 92
Old, Col William Donald 51, 89
Operations
Alpha (December 1944) 78, 80
Cotton Tail (December 1944) **(78)**79, 80, **81**
Grubworm (December 1944) 10, **(78)**79
Matterhorn (1944–45) 73–74, **(74)**75
Tsuzigiri (August – October 1943) 10, 40, **(65)66–67**, 68–69, **69**, 89
U-Go (March – June 1944) 10, **(70)**71, 72, 76, 77

performance and speed 13, 16, 17, **17**, 25, 26, **26**, 27, **27**, 55
pilot rotation 83, 85
postwar geopolitics in Asia 88
postwar surviving transport aircraft 91–92, **92**
POWs 29, **29**, 41
Product Line Maintenance 82–83

"Quit India" movement, the 55, 57

radar systems 22, 57
RAF, the 9, 49, 56, 64
rail traffic 20, **20**
Rape of Nanking, the 44
rate of fire 30–31
reconnaissance 55–56, **61**
repatriation of US troops, the 87
rescue and recovery 20, **69**, 91
Roosevelt, Franklin 6, 8, 9, 10, **33**, 34, 36, **36**, 38, 50, 54, 57–58, 62, 84
Roosevelt, Lt Franklin, Jr. **58**
Roosevelt, LtC Elliott **58**
Rosbert, C. J. 13
route structure **4**, **8**, **9**, 13, 17, 19–20, 22, 32, **35**, 36, 38, 44–45, **46**, 50, **50**, 51, **56**, **61**, **65**, 68, 69, 72, 73, 77, **78–79**, 83, **83**
Russo-Japanese War (1904–05), the 43

Second Sino-Japanese War, the 4–5, **5**, 6, **6**, 9, 31, **43**, 43–44, **45**, 78
Silk Road, the 45
Slim, Gen William 77
Smith, Brig Gen C. R. 57–58, **58**, 65
smoking and oxygen supply 77
Soong, T. V. 8, 9, 36, 37, 50
Soviet interests and actions 5, 43, 45, 48–49, 92
spare parts 18, 20, 37, 55, 62, 89
Stilwell, Gen Joseph 10, 36–37, 49, 50, 54, 57, 59, 62, **62**, 76, 80, 84
stone rollers **18**, 19

terrain factors 12, **13**, 19, 20, 33, 42–43, **46**, **48**, 51, 77
theater infrastructure 28, 36, 38, 42
trade embargo against Japan 8, 9, 48
training 62, **62**, 76
Trident Conference, the 10, 36–37, 62, 63, 64
Tripartite Pact, the 6, 9, 48
Truman, Harry 84
Tunner, Gen William 10, 76, **76**, 81–82, 83, 85, 87, **88**, 88–89

US Air Force Museum, the 92, **92**
US Army, the 73, 76, 77
5023rd Composite Group ("Merrill's Marauders") 19, 76
US interests and actions 6, 8, 9, 12, 18, 29, 33, 34–37, 38, 49, 50–55, **55**, 57–63, 64–65, **65**, 68–69, 73–77, **75**, 80, 84–86, **86**
and military aid to China 5, 10, 17, **33**, 34, 37, 42, 44, 48, 54, 84–85, 90
US Marines, the 74
US Navy Pacific Fleet, the 9, 29
USAAF (US Army Air Force), the 8, **12**, 16, 17, 18, 20, **49**, **50**, 54, 57, 58, 63, **65**, 74, 87, 88, 90
51st Fighter Group 55, 56
58th Very Heavy Bombardment Wing 76, 82
308th Bombardment Squadron **(65)66–67**, 68–69
Fourteenth Air Force 57, 62, **65**, **69**, 73, 78, 80, 89, **89**, 90
Search and Rescue Squadron 10, 65–68, **69**
Tenth Air Force 9, 10, 22, 50, 54, 57, 58, 59, 62, 69, 72, 73, 80, 89, **89**, 90
Twentieth Air Force 11, 73, 74, 78–80, 82, 88, **89**, 89–90

Vichy France 48

Wavell, Gen Archibald 64
weaponry 20–21, 25, **26**
7.7mm Type 89 machine gun (Japan) 25, 26, 27, 30, **30**, 31, 32, **65**
12.7mm Ho-103 machine gun (Japan) 25, 26, 27, 30–31, 32, **65**
.50cal machine gun (US) 21, 31, **(65)66–67**
Browning M2 .50 machine gun (US) 21, 30
Type 1 100kg bomb (Japan) 31
Type 92 250kg bomb (Japan) 31, **31**, 32
Type 92 500kg bomb (Japan) 31, **31**
Type 94 50kg bomb (Japan) 31, 32
weather conditions **13**, 19, 27, 38, 39, 40, 43, **46**, **51**, 55, 58, 63, 64, 68, 81
Wedemeyer, Gen Albert 10, 80